# MANAGING THE
# COMMANDING HEIGHTS

# MANAGING THE COMMANDING HEIGHTS

## NICARAGUA'S STATE ENTERPRISES

*Forrest D. Colburn*

UNIVERSITY OF CALIFORNIA PRESS

*Berkeley   Los Angeles   Oxford*

This book was written under the auspices
of the Center of International Studies,
Princeton University.

University of California Press
Berkeley and Los Angeles, California

University of California Press, Ltd.
Oxford, England

© 1990 by
The Regents of the University of California

**Library of Congress Cataloging-in-Publication Data**

Colburn, Forrest D.
    Managing the commanding heights : Nicaragua's state
enterprises /
    Forrest D. Colburn.
        p.   cm.
    Includes bibliographical references.
    ISBN 0-520-06759-2 (alk. paper)
    1. Government business enterprises—Nicaragua.   2.
Government   ownership—Nicaragua.   3. Industry and
state—Nicaragua.   4. Land,   Nationalization of—
Nicaragua.   5. Agriculture—Economic aspects—
Nicaragua.   I. Title.
    HD4038.C65   1990
    338.9669—dc20                                          89-37514
                                                               CIP

Printed in the United States of America

1   2   3   4   5   6   7   8   9

The paper used in this publication meets the minimum
requirements of American National Standard for
Information Sciences—Permanence of Paper for Printed
Library Materials, ANSI Z39.48-1984.   ∞

*I am grateful to those friends and colleagues who helped me in Managua, Havana, Princeton, Addis Ababa, and Bern. My greatest debt, though, is to the peasants and workers in rural Nicaragua who consented to speak with me.*

no somos aves para vivir del aire
no somos peces para vivir del mar
somos hombres para vivir de la tierra
　　　　—Bernardino Díaz Ochon

# Contents

# Tables

# Introduction

In directing the construction and defense of the Soviet Union at its inception, Lenin argued not for nationalization of the entire economy but for nationalization of only the most important sectors of the economy, what he described as the "commanding heights." This suggestive phrase and the maxim behind it are one of Lenin's enduring legacies. Leaders of contemporary revolutions have followed the practice of nationalization and state management of the commanding heights. Most revolutionary elites have been at least loosely inspired by Lenin and the program he articulated to transform Russia. But even when revolutionary elites have not been so inspired—as in Iran—they too have sought to nationalize key sectors of the economy, whether they be diamond mines or sugar estates. Nationalization is invariably the most consequential economic change in the initial postrevolutionary epoch and is held to be instrumental in the transition to some self-defined improved form of government.

This book explores the management of Nicaragua's commanding heights by the Sandinista National Liberation Front (FSLN), with an emphasis on the critical agrarian sector. On ending over forty years of rule by the Somozas in July 1979, the Sandinistas expropriated the extensive holdings of the Somoza family and of those intimately linked to the dictatorship. They confiscated over two thousand agricultural estates and enterprises, ranging from small farms to huge cattle ranches to sugar refineries and representing 25 percent of Nicaragua's land under cultivation and an even higher percentage of the processing of agricultural products. The Somozas' enormous investments—and the Sandinistas' endowment—in agriculture reflect the largely agrarian Nicaraguan economy. Eighty percent of exports, so necessary to a small state, are agricultural products. Despite continual migration to urban areas, the majority of Nicaraguans still earn their living from the land.

Also seized from the Somozas and their associates were one hundred thirty industrial or commercial enterprises, ranging from a cement factory to a Mercedes-Benz dealership. Foreign investments were not nationalized except for a handful of small gold mines owned by two companies, one American, the other Canadian. The Sandinistas further enhanced their influence over the Nicaraguan economy by nationalizing the country's banking and insurance systems and by placing all foreign trade under the control of state monopsonies. Finally, they conferred on themselves broad powers to regulate the private sector.

Private sector control over an estimated 65 percent of the Nicaraguan economy meant that from the beginning of Sandinista rule the outcome of many state initiatives depended on the dialectical performance of the state and countless economic actors. The regime was also constrained by the activities of the defeated "enemies of the revolution," by the vagaries of the international economy, and by international politics—in particular, relations with the "colossus to the north." Still, the consolidation of political power and the nationalization of property enabled the Sandinistas to implement, in diverse settings and locales, their vision of how civil society should be organized. The intentions of such efforts are significant. More important, though, is the state's demonstrated capacity to mobilize and deploy resources with the resolve and skill necessary to achieve outcomes it desires.

The argument advanced is dyadic: that the Sandinistas' bid to manage enterprises has been economically unsuccessful but politically successful. There are wrinkles though. First, while state enterprises are grossly inefficient, they produce. To use Schumpeter's analogy, economic performance resembles James Watt's first steam engine: it produced power, yet the piston wobbled loosely in the cylinder and hammered and pounded and hissed large quantities of wasted steam into the air. The inefficient management of Nicaragua's state enterprises is troublesome not only because it

dissipates scarce resources, but also because its marked inefficiency generates distortions throughout the economy, principally
by contributing to the debasement of currency. The inescapable
conclusion of the analysis is that the state sector has been anything
but the economic "vanguard." Instead, it weakens the economy,
exacerbating the exogenous constraints on the possibilities of radical change. Similarly, the poor economic performance of state
enterprises exacerbates, rather than alleviates, the structural obstacles to improving popular welfare.

Although state enterprises in Nicaragua are problematic economically, they are useful politically. They serve as a model, if
only a preliminary one, of how work should be organized, show-
ing especially how social relations within a firm should be dis-
tinct from those of the old order. They serve as a counterpoint to
the private sector, suggesting there is an alternative to private
management; by embodying the threat of nationalization, they
pressure private entrepreneurs and managers into at least superfi-
cially meeting state demands. Also, the state's willingness to inter-
cede economically deters intended or unintended sabotage by
members of the private sector who drag their feet or abandon
their enterprises. More immediately, the enterprises serve as outposts of the state, especially useful in isolated areas. As branches
of the government they can facilitate the provision of services,
from medical care, to transportation for visiting officials, to food
for soldiers. Finally, state enterprises give the local population
patronage-like benefits, principally employment. Recipients are a
captive audience for governmental propaganda and directives.
Thus, state enterprises provide a host of political advantages or,
in other words, political strength to a new regime—a regime that
is ambitious, but inexperienced and confronted with enemies.

The wrinkle in the political contribution of state enterprises is
that their invariable inefficiency, usually manifested through financial losses, can be an embarrassment. General economic woes
and specific instances of incompetence can erode the legitimacy
of a postrevolutionary regime. In Nicaragua this phenomenon is
most visibly illustrated by the well-known joke that the designated acronym of the state sector, APP, stands not for *área de
propiedad del pueblo* but *autorizado para perder* (not "property
of the people" but "authorized to be unprofitable"). Still, al-

though the loss of legitimacy stemming from economic inefficiency may be significant, economic performance is only one of
the many factors that influence a regime's legitimacy. The perceived alternative—the private sector—may for different reasons
enjoy even less legitimacy. Equally important, political problems
engendered by economic inefficiency are general and dispersed,
whereas the political benefits of state enterprises are more immediate and locale-bound.

Documenting the role of state enterprises in postrevolutionary
Nicaragua is not especially difficult. Explaining outcomes, however, is more elusive, especially if functional explanations are
eschewed. Nonetheless, this study attempts to be both theoretical
and empirical, with the conviction that the relevance of theory is
best demonstrated in the specificity of analysis. An awareness of
theoretical considerations informs empirical work; good theoretical work takes place in conjunction with empirical study. Both
are essential.

## Mode of Inquiry

How the state manages the commanding heights has
implications for popular welfare, state making, and the power of
the revolutionary elite. Students of contemporary revolutions
have, however, slighted this issue of state capacity to emphasize
instead state autonomy and the constraints, especially the international constraints, on revolutionary change. Their emphasis reflects academic fashion as well as the importance of state autonomy and its relative methodological tidiness compared to the
study of state capacity.

Studying state autonomy is the easier approach because it
concentrates on structural variables, in particular economic indices of strength and advantage. At the extreme, it holds that
structural constraints determine political outcomes. Such an approach is wrong. Even in small, poor countries, politics is the
outcome of choices within constraints. Choices embody an element of freedom, constraints one of necessity. Correspondingly,
while postrevolutionary regimes do have limited autonomy, they
can marshal and employ available resources as they see fit, to
restructure society within the imposed parameters. This effort

may involve an attack on the parameters, or at least a bid to alter them.

The three basic premises of this work are that structural constraints do not completely determine the actions taken by the leaders of revolutionary regimes; that within the set of feasible actions compatible with all the constraints, leaders choose those they believe will bring the best results; and that decisions are made without knowledge of their consequences. The broad implication of these premises suggests that to understand the patterns of change in poor countries, more attention should be paid to the capacity for autonomous choice on the part of local actors.

Explaining choices calls for a familiarity with the context and, above all, careful selection of the unit of analysis. The focus here is on individual motivations and actors. This emphasis affords a number of advantages. First, and most important, it encourages the search for intentional instead of simply functional explanations.[1] Second, it encourages the linkage of microlevel behavior to macrolevel behavior and vice versa. Third, it demands specific delineation of the interplay between the context of decisions and the decisions themselves. Fourth, it guards against the common fallacy of reification in the study of politics.

In keeping with the aspirations of the book and the mode of inquiry adopted, the study is divided into three parts. The first part draws on the experience of similarly situated postrevolutionary regimes to describe typical outcomes of nationalization and state management of the commanding heights. It attempts to delineate trends and tensions and, to the extent possible, to offer an explanation for patterns of behavior that recur across cases.

Part Two opens with an overview of the Sandinistas' nationalization of important segments of Nicaragua's economy and of the choices made by the revolutionary elite. The body of Part Two gives a detailed description of three state enterprises that represent the range of experiences encountered in the vital agrarian sector. A chapter is devoted to each firm. The Enterprise Oscar Turcios is typical in that it is poorly managed and loses a great deal of money; located in northern Nicaragua, it produces

---

1. Jon Elster, *Explaining Technical Change* (Cambridge: Cambridge University Press, 1983), p. 23.

tobacco. The Enterprise Camilo Ortega, named after the mar-
tyred brother of comandantes Daniel and Humberto Ortega, is
the most successful state enterprise in Nicaragua; it is located in
the center of Nicaragua's populous Pacific region and cultivates
cotton. In a war zone (on the Costa Rican border), the Enterprise
Commander Marcos Somarriba raises cattle along the banks of
the San Juan River. Together these three case studies offer a rich
interpretative setting for adumbrating the multitude of factors
shaping the capacity of a postrevolutionary state.

The third part of the book uses the microlevel data presented
in Part Two, coupled with similar data from other Nicaraguan
state enterprises, to explain consequential macrolevel issues. It
pays particular attention to the relation of state enterprises to
other economic and political actors, including the state itself.
The analysis concludes with a critique of the role of state enterprises in revolutionary change in poor countries.

## Sources of Data

The data for this study on Nicaragua come from an eight-
month consulting assignment with the Office of Enterprise Management in the Nicaraguan Ministry of Agricultural Development
and Agrarian Reform (MIDINRA). The consultation was conducted under the auspices of the Central American Institute of
Business Administration (INCAE) from January to August 1985.
The ministry requested assistance in promoting efficiency within
the productive entities under its responsibility, organized into 102
enterprises, most of which are conglomerates of farms, agro-
industrial complexes, and service and commercial establishments.

The focus of the effort with the enterprises was on cost control and evaluation, but those questions could not be isolated
from broader concerns, including overt political issues. Problems
ultimately addressed ranged from the calculation of depreciation
for cannibalized tractors, to incentives, to relations with other
governmental bureaucracies. Collaborating with the ministry's
Office of Enterprise Management entailed regular visits to individual enterprises and work on a national level at the ministry's
central office in Managua.

Most of the data come from MIDINRA in the form of published and unpublished documents and interviews with its many and diverse employees. Augmenting these data are published and unpublished documents from other branches of the Nicaraguan government and, to a much lesser extent, from nongovernmental organizations.

In general, the data pose few problems of reliability or validity. Thus, they are used with confidence and without recourse to multiple sources. MIDINRA's statistics on agricultural production present numerous difficulties, in part because they attempt to measure the performance of the private sector, including peasants. However, MIDINRA's quantitative data (especially financial) on the ministry's activities cause few problems because the data have a more limited scope and in most cases the banking system corroborates them. Narrative discussions in MIDINRA's internal reports are often not thorough, but they are candid.

Interviews with employees of individual state enterprises are also largely free of problems. Except at the Enterprise Commander Marcos Somarriba (chapter 5), interviews were usually conducted in the presence of, or with, an official of MIDINRA's central office in Managua. Respondents appeared to speak openly, even willing, for example, to criticize MIDINRA's central office or the leadership of their particular enterprise. Interviews were loosely structured around a continuously evolving written set of questions. The kind of answers solicited, however, were not amenable to generating interval data. Instead, interviews were used to build an interpretative foundation to worry through the state sector's configuration of problems and successes.

## Limits of the Study

The principal limitation of the book, aside from the deliberate narrowness of its subject, is temporal. Nicaragua's state enterprises are analyzed at one moment in the metamorphosis of the country's revolution. While much attention is paid to detail, it is done to elucidate enduring issues and not to give definitive form to a static phenomenon. Politics has to be understood as a temporal sequence of events, not as a moment in time.

There are two other major limitations of the study. First, the attempt in chapter 1 to illuminate Nicaragua's experience through a comparative review of similarly situated regimes is only suggestive, given the considerable methodological difficulties of cross-national comparison. Such an exercise is nonetheless fruitful because it suggests that Nicaragua's dilemmas are not atypical. Second, the economic data employed in the study are more persuasive than the data about politics. That imbalance seems to bedevil studies exploring the interplay of economics and politics, but every effort has been made to compensate for it.

# PART ONE

# 1

## Postrevolutionary State Enterprises

The locus of revolutions since World War II has been in poor countries, where states have traditionally been weak, the populace largely rural, and, except in mining enclaves, the economy agricultural. Examples include China, Vietnam, Bolivia, Algeria, Cuba, Cambodia, Ethiopia, Guinea-Bissau, Angola, Mozambique, Iran, and Nicaragua. These revolutions have been engendered by misery and exploitation. However, revolutions have seemingly been possible only when these conditions could be popularly attributed to an unrepresentative government whose shortcomings and excesses were easily personified. When revolutionaries triumph, the interdependence of economics and politics continues. Changes in political power and in the institutions that manifest it are necessary for broad-based economic development. And economic improvements—particularly for the disenfranchised—are needed to support, consolidate, and defend new political institutions.

In their bids to build new political institutions, redress economic inequities, and alleviate poverty, revolutionary elites confront numerous obstacles. Some are common to all poor countries where material scarcity dictates the parameters of innovation. In addition, technical and administrative skills are limited in the labor force. Often such nation-states depend on exports of one or two primary products and are vulnerable to the structure and dynamics of international markets.

11

Other obstacles are inherent to revolutionary regimes. There is material damage from the insurrection itself. Numerous implicit social contracts, from work norms to relations among ethnic groups, are ruptured, often with costly consequences. Finally, emergent regimes face opposition and subversion from defeated political forces and social strata threatened by postrevolutionary change.

To accomplish their objectives, revolutionary elites invariably increase the central government's authority, especially in economic affairs. For ideological, political, and pragmatic reasons, the state seeks dominance over the economy. It becomes the planner of development, the catalyst for economic growth, and the arbiter of distribution. It nationalizes the most important and concentrated centers of production as well as the houses of capital, commerce, and foreign trade. In most poor countries, however, the technical and managerial capacity to nationalize all assets does not exist. The lack of feasibility or desirability of the government's assuming complete responsibility for economic production leads to a serious problem with nationalization: how to carry it out without disrupting the willingness to invest and produce in what is often the substantial part of the economy remaining in the private sector.[1] Through both overt and tacit resistance, private producers from the entire spectrum of the economy are able to restrict state autonomy.

There are many forms of strife in postrevolutionary regimes, from jockeying within the ruling elite, to ethnic schisms, to open counterrevolutions. One of the most widespread and persistent kinds of political strife, though, is the tension between the state and private economic actors, from foreign capitalists to retailers to peasant householders. The state regularly announces its plans and aspirations, cajoles private enterprises into meeting them, and belittles any failure. Private enterprises, for their part, are less able—and perhaps less inclined—to publicize their cooperation, acquiescence, foot dragging, or open sabotage. Still, the state itself maintains an ongoing public transcript of the dialectical relation between the public and the private. This transcript

1. David Morawetz, "Economic Lessons from Some Small Socialist Developing Countries," *World Development* 8 (May–June 1980): 354–355.

provides scholars with a window into many of the possibilities and problems of postrevolutionary society.

Less discussed by the state, and at times hidden, is the management of the public sector. While postrevolutionary regimes in poor countries do not, at least initially, have the resources to assume complete responsibility for their economies, they do tend to take over the famed "commanding heights." In small, poor countries, these commanding heights are different from those Lenin captured. There are no steel mills. But those enterprises that do meet the strategic needs of the economy, such as the generation of foreign exchange, are targeted for nationalization. How these enterprises are administered is consequential, and at times decisive. Perhaps because the management of the public sector does not occasion overt political strife—or at least does not require a dialogue—there is only a limited public transcript of what is done and why.

Nonetheless, what the state takes on and how it manages its economic enterprises have importance for a number of reasons. First, the state often assumes responsibility for key activities, including those generating foreign exchange, those most technically sophisticated, and those providing a crucial service or product either to the populace at large or to other enterprises. Second, the state often devotes considerable—at times disproportionate—attention and resources to its enterprises. Third, state enterprises, especially those in service industries, often have a major impact on the performance of private enterprises. Fourth, and most important, state enterprises are assumed to be the "vanguard" of the economy—a model of how the economy is to develop in the transition to some self-defined improved form of government, invariably socialism. The political and economic nuances of state administration shape postrevolutionary change. Ultimately, state *capacity* is likely to be as consequential as (though perhaps less noticed than) state *autonomy* in determining the success of postrevolutionary society. And state capacity is likely to prove more malleable, to offer more choices, to the revolutionary leadership.

Comparing and contrasting the disparate information available on state management of economic enterprises in postrevolutionary regimes is both complex and problematic. Nonetheless, reviewing the experience of countries as diverse as China, Cuba,

Ethiopia, and Mozambique suggests a common sequence of intentions, decisions, constraints, and outcomes. The sequence is best conceptualized not as linear but as circular: outcomes in their turn lead to both decisions and constraints on those decisions.

State enterprises in contemporary postrevolutionary regimes are inextricably linked to politics. These economic entities are used in numerous ways, some of them conflicting, as political instruments. At the onset they are used to smash or at least arrest the old order. Concomitantly, they are used to propagate desired political values—to identify them as the antithesis of the former regime and as the bearer of a new order. More concretely, state enterprises are strategically located branches of the government that command resources necessary for a panoply of tasks, from providing social services to mustering recruits for political demonstrations and, in extreme cases, for armies. In this capacity, state enterprises can be used to reward supporters, both tacit and overt, of the revolution. To fulfill these and other political tasks, state enterprises are extremely useful, usually more so than traditional ministries and government agencies. No contemporary revolutionary elite, faced with the necessity of consolidating power, has resisted the temptation to use economic entities as political instruments.

Yet state enterprises remain economic entities, indeed often the most important and expensive enterprises in impoverished nations. Meeting political objectives entails a high cost, not just in direct materials but also, through a slighting of economic criteria, a significant but less measurable cost in opportunity. In a postrevolutionary epoch to manage most enterprises efficiently and profitably is a daunting task. Markets for inputs are disrupted, work norms are in abeyance, skilled labor is often scarce, and markets for finished products or services are often either controlled or depressed. The call for state enterprises to assist in political tasks, though, makes for an even more difficult economic environment, one where problems are not tackled aggressively. Instead, the focus is on meeting political goals, oblique as they may be.

The economic cost of state enterprises tends to become an intolerable burden. Investments of scarce resources yield little economic return. And whereas the labor force of state enterprises is easily mobilized for political purposes, in time the typical economic inefficiency of state enterprises can make them political liabilities. Not only can state enterprises place an economic burden on a nation's budget, they can weaken a regime's legitimacy. Exhausted political tools can become a political embarrassment.

In postrevolutionary regimes, the degree of political pressure to which enterprises are subject shifts with the national economy and with the ideology and political strength of the ruling elite. China and Cuba, for instance, each underwent five marked changes in management style during their first twenty years of postrevolutionary rule.[2] In China the oscillations were accompanied by a "red versus expert" debate. In Cuba there was less discussion. Remarkably, at comparable periods in their revolutionary development, China and Cuba have had different attitudes toward state enterprises. This divergence, and the continued reversals in each country, suggest that there is no gradual evolution of state management of the economy. Rather, there is commitment to a course of action fraught with contradictions that cannot be resolved but can only be accommodated.

These ambiguities and contradictions are reproduced at the level of the individual enterprise. Directors are presented with multiple demands. Typically they are told to produce efficiently but in a socially or politically responsible way. Perhaps left unsaid is that they are to cooperate with local representatives of the government; if they do not, they may become embroiled in conflict. In these circumstances it is a rational outcome for the enterprise to be unprofitable, as its administration tries to comply at least in part with all demands. On the contrary, it is all but irrational for the director to challenge the implicit political demands upon the firm in an effort to be economically efficient and profitable. Economic goals give way with relative ease. The triumph of politics over economics is reinforced because the benefits of meeting political demands are local and likely to spread over many actors, whereas the immediate benefits of economic

2. Franz Schurmann, *Ideology and Organization in Communist China* (Berkeley: University of California Press, 1968), 4; Carmelo Mesa-Lago, *The Economy of Socialist Cuba: A Two-Decade Appraisal* (Albuquerque: University of New Mexico Press, 1981).

efficiency usually go elsewhere, often to a single government entity. Efficiency comes to be close to a "public good," with the classic inappropriate incentives for hard-pressed individuals.

Capitalist nation-states, especially poor ones, have also employed state enterprises. Here too the enterprises have been manipulated for political purposes, contributing to a common absence of profitability. On first impression, state enterprises in postrevolutionary regimes may be distinguished from their counterparts in capitalist regimes only in that they are subject to greater political manipulation and that their financial performance is consequently more problematic. That beguiling appearance of similarity, however, neglects the different role that state enterprises play in revolutionary regimes, which are usually socialist.

In capitalist countries, state enterprises are part of a strategy of economic development. Although state enterprises are often used for political tasks, they are not essential for the regime's raison d'être, legitimacy, or political survival and thus can be phased out or turned over to private entrepreneurs and managers. And the capitalist regime's stability is not threatened.

By contrast, in postrevolutionary regimes, which are inherently vulnerable and unstable, state enterprises are an integral and inviolable part. They help define and protect radical change. Socialism, after all, is characterized by the socialization of property. Revolution entails overthrowing not just political elites but economic elites too. If remnants of the economic elite survive, as they often do, state enterprises can help limit their ability to undermine revolutionary change. When a regime such as that of Cuba has surmounted its initial years of postrevolutionary rule and consolidated power, state enterprises may no longer be part of the defense of the revolutionary project. But they continue to be important in distinguishing it from the former regime and from neighboring capitalist countries. They provide incentives to continue revolutionary transformations, as well as support for revolutionary leadership.

The roles state enterprises take in postrevolutionary regimes are enhanced by the latitude emergent leaders have in deciding how to organize and manage them. They prove hospitable to the revolutionary *mentalité*, which discredits all those associated with the old order and offers promises to others formerly exploited and marginalized. In an environment of multiple constraints, state enterprises offer leaders a visible margin of autonomy.

Using state enterprises for key political tasks generates economic problems of inefficiency and distortion in factors and currency. Yet because state enterprises are instrumental to post-revolutionary regimes, their management cannot be left to "the discipline of the market," as is an option in capitalist countries. And postrevolutionary regimes may be less able to shoulder losses of efficiency in key sectors of the economy than their capitalist counterparts.

The specific import of state enterprises for revolutionary change varies from case to case. Reviewing the experience of state enterprises in contemporary postrevolutionary cases suggests the range of possibilities and generalities.

## Establishing State Enterprises

Accompanying every revolution since World War II has been an expansion in the state's economic role, including the management of enterprises. Nationalization begins immediately on the seizure of power, confiscating the commanding heights of the economy and the property of the principal enemy (or enemies) of the revolution. Often the two are the same, or nearly so. This initial wave of nationalization gives the new regime substantial, but incomplete, control over the economy. As the following account of Iran suggests, an increase in the state's responsibilities is likely to be the most consequential economic change immediately after the seizure of power:

> The revolution led to considerable disruption and to far-reaching changes in the structure of the Iranian economy. In the short term, industrial activity declined and there was a shift away from industry and toward trade and commerce. Various land distribution schemes proved abortive; yet the pattern of private ownership in agriculture was disturbed and agricultural production suffered. The central planning machinery broke down, and the Plan and Budget Organization (PBO) lost control over the expenditures of the ministries and government agencies. Some measures were

adopted to ameliorate the lot of the poor and to spread economic opportunities. But these had only limited impact. More significantly, the government took over large sectors of the economy through nationalization and expropriation, including banking, insurance, major industry, large-scale agriculture and construction, and an important part of foreign trade. It also involved itself in the domestic distribution of goods. As a result, the economic role of the state was greatly swollen and that of the private sector greatly diminished by the revolution.[3]

This account, attaching the significance to state nationalization, generally fits other cases.

Variances among countries in the amount and kind of property nationalized in the initial phase can be ascribed in large measure to the strength of various economic sectors and their relation to the deposed elite. As nationalization continues, more significant, and less easily explained, differences arise in its extent and pace. In China and Cuba, nationalization of the economy continued apace: in China it was complete in seven years, and in Cuba nearly so in nine years (30 percent of the agricultural sector remained the only exception).[4] A notable contrast has occurred in countries such as Angola, Mozambique, Ethiopia, Nicaragua, and Iran. Here nationalizations have continued but at a much slower pace, often only in response to problems arising in individual private enterprises. The most striking slowdown in nationalizations is in Ethiopia. In this predominantly agrarian economy, after a dozen years of postrevolutionary rule only 5 percent of cultivated land is held by state farms.[5] Of course, state control of the economy can be accomplished other than through outright ownership and management, but Ethiopia's experience suggests that the strong trend toward nationalization in postrevolutionary regimes may be tempered by problems encountered in the transition to a new order.

3. Shaul Bakhash, *The Reign of the Ayatollahs: Iran and the Islamic Revolution* (New York: Basic Books, 1984), p. 166.

4. Schurmann, *Ideology and Organization,* pp. xxvii–xxviii, 57; Arthur MacEwan, *Revolution and Economic Development in Cuba* (New York: St. Martin's Press, 1981), p. 70.

5. Keith Griffin and Roger Hay, "Problems of Agricultural Development in Socialist Ethiopia: An Overview and a Suggested Strategy," *Journal of Peasant Studies* 13 (1985): 54.

Fathoming the propensity of revolutionary elites to national-ize property is instrumental in understanding how state enter-prises, once constituted, perform. There are a number of possible explanations, many of them reinforcing, for this desire to see the state assume economic responsibilities. With the departure of the former elite there is often no alternative, as was true in the luso-phone countries in Africa. In such cases only the state has the necessary organizational capacity, access to financing, and, per-haps, access to foreign technical assistance. Also, the state can tolerate risks that would likely deter the most capable and well endowed private enterprise.

Yet in many cases private actors, both domestic and foreign, may continue their erstwhile activities or assume the manage-ment of abandoned or confiscated enterprises. Even in cases where this strategy is technically and politically feasible, how-ever, there is still a pronounced preference for state administra-tion. At times the preference can be explained by the perceived public nature of either the service provided, such as utilities, or the resources employed, such as lumber or minerals. Regimes of every bent employ this logic to justify public enterprises.

There remain, however, many decisions to employ the state that cannot be explained solely by the lack of an alternative or by the criterion of the public good. The state often intervenes in the economy because the ruling elite frankly believes that to do so is politically desirable and useful and perceives ideological goals and the consolidation of power as being in harmony. In such instances it is difficult to delineate the precise origin and inten-tions of state policies, but revolutionary elites do appear to base decisions both on ideological predispositions and on pragmatic concerns about maintaining their power.

Except in the Iranian case, the leadership of all contemporary postrevolutionary regimes has been drawn to the tenets of Marxism-Leninism. Many leaders and well-positioned cadres are versed in the prolific writings of Marx, Engels, and Lenin. Yet the contribution of Marxism-Leninism appears more to suggest gen-eral aspirations and, much less, guidelines on how to achieve them than to detail policy prescriptions. The aspirations of triumphant revolutionaries are not unlike those found in any country: eco-nomic independence from foreign interests, economic growth and equality, and the provision for basic needs. What distinguishes postrevolutionary regimes is in part their greater commitment to economic equality but, more important, the means they use to reach their goals. They commonly accept the legitimacy and efficacy of the state and, more generally, of public forms of management. Concomitantly, they disdain and suspect private initiative. They share a belief in the malleability of economics, in its progress, and a commitment to economies of scale and technology.

Although revolutionary leaders are invariably drawn to the ideology, and even the phraseology and iconography, of Marxism-Leninism, they appear to understand little of Marxist regimes' concrete experience, either in the Soviet Union or more similarly situated countries in the Third World. Consequently, they remain unaware of the everyday administrative and organizational tasks involved in implementing Marxism-Leninism. The ambiguities of Marx's and Lenin's writings go unappreciated, as do the ways in which those ambiguities can be—and have been—used to justify a wide range of economic decisions, some in contradiction with one another.

At times it appears that Marxism-Leninism and the more general concept of socialism are important in providing a model antithetical to that of capitalism, which invariably is equated with the hated old order. As one of the Nicaraguan comandantes remarked, "We have seen capitalism (in Nicaragua), and we do not want it."[6] Marxism-Leninism provides a coherent critique of capitalism, an antithetical development model, and a rationale for the new leaders to entrench themselves in power. Perhaps Islam performs the same functions in Iran.[7]

As attractive and useful as Marxism-Leninism is to revolutionary leaderships, this doctrine gives government no specificity. For example, it does not suggest how to manage a ministry, a bank, an army, or an enterprise. It likewise says nothing about such mundane but consequential concerns as growth of the money supply, taxation, or income policies. Marxism-Leninism is thus more a mentalité than a coherent and all-encompassing ideology. This is not an idle distinction but points to the inert, obscure, uncon-

---

6. Jaime Wheelock, conversation, Managua, May 1985.
7. Such a role is suggested in Bakhash, *Reign of the Ayatollahs*.

scious elements in a given worldview. It appears to explain the millenarian ideas among revolutionary elites in the Third World.

The consequences of chiliastic mentalités among individual decision makers are important. Their central political concern comes to be the transformation of individual preferences, rather than their aggregation. Both the attempt to transform preferences and the ambiguity of the intended transformation introduce considerable uncertainty into decision making. This uncertainty plagues both leadership and low-level administrators.

Although decisions to employ and extend the state in the management of the economy are inspired by mentalités, they often concretely respond to pressing problems and threats. The most common problem is the production and requisition of needed goods—food, consumer products, or commodities that earn foreign exchange. Thus, for example, the rapid expansion of state farms in Ethiopia is explained, "in order to meet the growing shortages of grain in the urban areas and the raw material supply of the country's major manufacturing industries."[8] The provision of foodstuffs, especially at low cost, and the generation of foreign exchange to pay for imports can be crucial in meeting the consumption needs of those loyal to the revolution, including cadres, and of those groups whose support is deemed important, such as residents of the capital.

States often intervene in the economy to maintain existing levels of production or accumulation in economic enclaves established under the old order. Likewise, the state establishes its enterprises selectively and employs in them the capital goods that it is able to receive from international trade, credit, or assistance. For example, in Mozambique the Front for the Liberation of Mozambique (FRELIMO) established state farms on the commercial farms abandoned by Portuguese settlers and subsequently allocated to them the bulk of imported farm machinery and other agricultural inputs.[9] Its intention was to maintain and, when possible, to extend economies of scale and improved technology.

8. Ministry of State Farms Development, untitled report (Addis Ababa, 1985, Mimeographed), p. 1.
9. Joseph Hanlon, *Mozambique: The Revolution Under Fire* (London: Zed Press, 1984), pp. 84, 100–102.

At times the state intercedes because of apprehension about turning over productive entities to either laborers or peasants. The apprehension is not just that economies of scale may be lost but also that what is produced may be consumed locally, thus disrupting the flow of goods and services to other sectors, including the state itself. Also, access to property and capital—especially if it occurs unequally—may foster social inequities and engender antirevolutionary behavior. The influential Cuban statesman Carlos Rafael Rodríguez concurs in the view that distributing land to individuals buttresses capitalism: "The small landholder promotes capitalism, hour by hour, minute by minute."[10]

In summary, there are multiple motivations for state management of certain key enterprises. Delineating the relative importance of each cause is especially difficult because many overlap or are mutually reinforcing. What is clear, though, is that the causes are inherently political. In no case is the decision for state intervention in the economy based on narrow economic criteria, on calculations of costs and benefits. Politics is paramount.

Yet exactly what constitutes the politically correct decision at any given intersection remains unclear. Ambiguities accompany the revolutionaries' chiliastic mentalité, and uncertainty stems from attempts to reconcile their ideological preferences with pragmatic considerations. Even when decisions are taken, they are necessarily under review and revision forever.

## Performance

The performance of state enterprises in contemporary postrevolutionary regimes is ambiguous. In the most basic task—production of goods and services—the evidence is mixed. State enterprises do produce as mandated, even under the most adverse conditions. And what is produced is easily requisitioned. Yet often, production targets are not met, and in fact yields are often inferior to those of private producers. This pattern is neatly

10. Carlos Rafael Rodríguez, *Letra con filo*, vol. 2 (Havana: Editorial de Ciencias Sociales, 1983), p. 397.

demonstrated in Ethiopia. A governmental report on the country's state farms concluded that targeted yields were not being met:

> Even though it has been demonstrated through research results that average yields should for corn be over 50 qts, for wheat over 28 qts and for fiber crops about 26 qts and over 150 for fruits and vegetables, these farms have gravitated around 27 qts for corn, 15 qts for wheat, 21 qts for cotton, and 104 and 56 qts for fruits and vegetables when compared with planned outputs.[11]

Not only have Ethiopian state farms produced less than planned, they have also produced less than the private sector. Indeed, evidence suggests that yields of coffee and pulse in the peasant sector are at least 50 percent greater than in the state farm sector.[12]

Other postrevolutionary regimes in Africa have experienced roughly similar results. In China and Cuba collectivization proceeded so quickly that there is no comparative basis for measuring yields of state enterprises. In both cases goods and services were produced, but often below targeted levels. Yet it is difficult to measure how realistic stated objectives were, and whether estimates were sound or inflated in a bid to stimulate administrators. The Nicaraguan case is more illuminating because state enterprises have coexisted with private enterprises. Here the results have been more satisfactory than in Ethiopia. For example, while the yields of Nicaraguan state farms have regularly been below those set by the Ministry of Agricultural Development and Agrarian Reform, they have—on the whole—been equal to, or only slightly less than, those of the private sector.[13]

Where uniformity occurs in the performance of state enterprises is in their financial losses. Seemingly without exception, state enterprises lose considerable sums of money, thus posing a burden on the state and ultimately on the polity. In many in-

---

11. Ministry of State Farms Development, report, p. 17.
12. Griffin and Hay, "Problems of Agricultural Development," p. 60.
13. Comparing aggregate yields is difficult because the private sector has a much wider variety of producers in size of holdings and sophistication of technology employed. However, even the principal organization in the Nicaraguan private sector acknowledges that yields on state farms have been respectable (see Union of Nicaraguan Agricultural Producers [UPANIC], "Estudios económicos" [Managua, 1983, Mimeographed]).

. stances these losses and the burdens that result are stunning. A representative characterization comes from the Ethiopian government's report:

> the performance of most enterprises has not been encouraging and . . . their liquidity position is very precarious. Most of these enterprises have sustained huge losses during that period thus adding to the already large accumulated deficits brought forward from prior periods.[14]

In Mozambique, after six years of postrevolutionary rule, the Ministry of Agriculture admitted that not one state farm was profitable.[15] After the same period in Nicaragua, only four state farms (out of 102) were profitable.[16]

Cuba's experience suggests that the propensity of state enterprises to generate losses is profound and difficult to reverse through increased output of goods and services. In Cuba, after two decades of experiment in organization and technology, state farms have expanded production through increased yields, especially in the case of the country's most important crop—sugar.[17] Yet at the Third Party Congress (celebrated after twenty-seven years of postrevolutionary rule), Fidel Castro publicly bemoaned the losses of state enterprises. He even asserted that losses had recently increased.[18]

As a result of the financial losses of state enterprises, this significant sector is anything but an economic catalyst. Indeed, instead of being the "vanguard" of a booming economy, they are invariably a drag on the economy, as their significant losses worsen the dire economic status of contemporary postrevolutionary regimes. The losses of state farms not only contribute directly to economic problems, especially inflation, but also often represent a cost in

14. Ministry of State Farms Development, report, p. 32.
15. Hanlon, *Mozambique,* p. 101.
16. Conversation with officials of the Ministry of Agricultural Development and Agrarian Reform (MIDINRA), February 1985. Aggregate financial data on MIDINRA's enterprises is presented in MIDINRA, "Evaluación financiera de las empresas de reforma agraria, ciclo 1983–1984" (Managua, 1984, Mimeographed).
17. Brian Pollitt, "The Transition to Socialist Agriculture in Cuba: Some Salient Features," *IDS Bulletin* 13 (1982): 20.
18. *Granma Weekly Review,* 14 December 1986.

opportunities: scarce resources entrusted to state enterprises might have been more productively employed elsewhere.

The poor financial performance of state enterprises creates indirect political problems too, ones more difficult to measure. First, the local perception that state enterprises are poorly managed and that the capacity of the state does not meet its own expectations weakens the legitimacy of the regime. Second, economic problems create inconveniences and hardships for consumers and thus contribute to political dissatisfaction. Both problems affect the populace at large, including the stated beneficiaries of the revolution— the poor and the dispossessed. If a revolution is besieged by a counterrevolution, as is common at least in the initial years, these problems can be dangerous. It is a truism of both revolutionary and counterrevolutionary insurgency that success depends on generating some popular support, or at least the tacit support of those disaffected with the existing regime.

Despite these difficulties, it is a mistake to conclude from the financial losses of state enterprises that they, and the more general phenomenon of state involvement in the economy, are a failure. One paradox of contemporary postrevolutionary regimes is that they are on the whole politically stable despite poor—and at times disastrous—economic performance. State enterprises help to explain this paradox. Whereas the economic costs and benefits of state enterprises may be clear, the political costs and benefits are more ambiguous. Despite the aforementioned political costs, there are many political benefits to extensive state control of the economy. Most political benefits come from patronage and often contribute directly to the enterprises' poor financial performance through over-staffing, lax labor discipline, channeling resources to political activities, and setting low prices for goods and services produced (especially if they are destined for popular consumption). Ironically, the state can garner political support (and control) by alleviating economic problems to which it itself contributes. Here rationing is the example par excellence.

Thus, in the management of state enterprises, economic logic and political logic clash. Yet the apparent negative correlation between economic efficiency and political goals is neither strong nor stable. Under any circumstances in the aftermath of an insurrection, economic efficiency and growth would be elusive. Administrators confront a daunting array of obstacles that, in the enthusiasm of seizing power, they had probably not anticipated: labor indiscipline, the absence of trained personnel, shortages of inputs and machinery, and general chaos. Revolutionary leaders undoubtedly believe at the moment of their triumph that they can fulfill their economic and political ambitions simultaneously. But relatively quickly they must face a tradeoff between the unbridled pursuit of political goals and the attainment of economic efficiency and growth. This tradeoff further muddies decision making.

The elusiveness of economic gains, particularly with political change, presents revolutionary leaders with several problems. In addition to making decisions with considerable uncertainty, they must pursue multiple objectives (here dyadically summarized as political and economic) that are not necessarily complementary. Furthermore, even short-term outcomes depend on the largely unpredictable interplay of numerous actors, including those hostile to political change. The revolutionary leaders do not pursue their agenda in a vacuum. Finally, the whole gamut of decisions is forever constrained by powerful structures, principally by interested nations, the world economy, and inherited patterns of generating foreign exchange.

The ambiguity in decision making plagues the revolutionary elite, especially lower-level cadres and administrators—those who confront local peculiarities. For all decision makers there is likely to be no unique mode of behavior they can single out as the rational choice. They may rationally elect different courses, including the decision to muddle along, continually seeking the easiest course of action.

With formidable obstacles before those who must delineate clear and consistent action, other actors, including those supposedly being led, may be tempted to pursue their own narrow interests. They may be encouraged to act by a perception that the dispossessed have been "liberated" from authority and exploitation and are due to be rewarded with all they have been denied. Rational as such perceptions may be, they are devastating to a regime, committed to aiding the poor and yet confused about how to do so.

## Reform of State Enterprises

The invariable financial losses of state enterprises frequently make them the object of reform. At times these reforms are openly debated; at other times policy mandates and prescriptions are simply announced. In nearly all cases, though, there are powerful, if unspoken, political constraints on reform. The most basic appears to require that state assets continue to be managed as public goods. In many cases the leadership is unwilling to consider managing state enterprises in any other fashion, once they have been constituted as such. It is certainly unwilling to discuss transforming them into private enterprises. That tack would be decidedly—and embarrassingly—antirevolutionary.

Dissatisfaction with the financial performance of state enterprises may lead a regime, at most, to halt their formation or to restructure existing ones into another form of public entity—usually cooperatives. The case of Angola illustrates both outcomes. Confronted with the dismal performance of state coffee farms (which produced the country's most important agricultural export) and the general dismal state of the economy, the governing Popular Movement for the Liberation of Angola (MPLA) turned the state farms over to cooperatives composed of agricultural laborers.[19] Concurrently, the MPLA quietly set aside one of the goals announced immediately after seizing power—continued confiscation and nationalization.

Attempts to improve the management of state enterprises are likewise politically circumscribed. State enterprises must adhere to ill-defined revolutionary principles that are problematic to challenge—or even to clarify. Thus, efforts at reform often center on organizational structures, accounting standards, planning, and budgeting but exclude systems of incentive and discipline, social responsibilities, and articulating state enterprises with local communities and government bodies. Efforts at improving the management of state enterprises must take place within the limiting context of the government's political aspirations and pragmatic necessities.

19. Keith Somerville, *Angola* (London: Frances Pinter, 1986), p. 132.

At times, the policies that offer both efficient use of resources and profitability can undermine political goals, including egalitarianism and the use of economic entities to promote and maintain the power of the revolutionary elite. Bluntly put, promising reforms lead to a reverse, a return to the old order, to capitalism. They also often cause the retrenchment of the state and the strengthening of independent actors, both public and private. Thus the reforms, and those who advocate them, can appear counterrevolutionary. Equally troubling, halfway measures such as material incentives without "market discipline" often lead to profitability without efficiency. In such cases, of course, profits come only at the expense of others, be they consumers, other enterprises, or the government itself.

Fidel Castro's closing speech at Cuba's Third Party Congress captured many of these dilemmas:

> How were we going to solve our problems of material production and the country's development? Apparently, we thought that by dressing a person up as a capitalist we were going to achieve efficient production in the factory and so after a fashion we started to play at being capitalists. . . . And the characters dressed up as capitalists, many of our comrades dressed up as capitalists, began to act like capitalists, but without the capitalists' efficiency. Capitalists take better care of their factories and take better care of their money; they are always competing with other capitalists.[20]

Later in the same speech Castro referred to problems encountered with the liberalization of prices and the use of material bonuses:

> Naturally the problem of unprofitability was rather generalized, so wholesale prices of many products were raised and even this failed to make many enterprises profitable. . . . Generally speaking, they became increasingly unprofitable. The larger the salaries paid in that chaos of norms and more norms, bonuses and more bonuses, these administrators dressed up as capitalists could even start to compete among themselves to see who got the best workers, paid the best salaries, was less demanding and also played the

20. *Granma Weekly Review,* 14 December 1986.

role of populists, paternalists, what have you, making absolutely no demands, with all the consequences derived from this.[21]

Although Castro bemoans the populist and paternalist behavior of administrators, the Cuban regime has benefited from the popularity, or at least acquiescence, it has generated.

China and Cuba are the two contemporary postrevolutionary regimes that have both the most extensive and the most long-standing state participation in the economy. In the rich and occasionally colorful transcript of their debates on state management and its relation to building a new society, what is remarkable— especially given the many differences between the two countries— is the perennial tension between economics and politics. Too often, what is deemed politically desirable is economically problematic; what is economically pragmatic is politically unacceptable. The tension has been accommodated differently at various periods in each country, but in neither case has it been definitively resolved. Their experiences, especially juxtaposed, suggest how elusive are equity, efficiency, innovation, and growth under state supervision, and also the important ways in which economic management is constrained by politics.

## Conclusion

State control of the economy, down to the actual ownership and management of individual enterprises, has been a key feature of contemporary postrevolutionary regimes. It has yielded political dividends but has invariably resulted in serious economic problems that in time bring about a loss of political legitimacy. The gravity of economic inefficiency and disorder that may be traced to the state suggests that sheer administrative capacity, or lack thereof, is as much a constraint on the ability of revolutionary regimes to fulfill their material aspirations as are limits on state autonomy.

Given the economic problems posed by state management in

21. Ibid.

contemporary postrevolutionary regimes, it is hard to disagree with the conclusions of consulting advisers of the Soviet Gosplan attached to Ethiopia's Planning Ministry:

> Hasty and excessive conversion of economy into state property, whatever reasons may have dictated it, has often led to disorganization of economy and "rolling back" in the socio-political sphere.[22]

This conclusion, all the more remarkable because it comes from representatives of the most developed socialist country, could be extended to other contemporary postrevolutionary regimes, all of which are in poor countries.

It may seem persuasive but is ultimately facile to suggest that nationalization of the economy should not be hasty or excessive. Questions are left unanswered. If at least parts of the economy are to be nationalized, how can they be managed so as not to contribute to "disorganization of economy"? If a substantial part of the economy is to remain in private hands, what policies should the state adopt for these economic actors? Finally, if nationalization and state control of the economy have been instrumental in building new political institutions and maintaining political power, what alternative resources do revolutionary elites have? This last, more political, question is likely to be most meaningful and to shape, in large part, the economic guidelines for public and private enterprises.

22. Consulting Advisers of the USSR Gosplan, "Considerations on the Economic Policy of Ethiopia for the Next Few Years" (Addis Ababa, 1985, Mimeographed), p. 107 (the names of the Soviet advisers are listed on page 88 of the document).

# PART TWO

# 2

# Nationalization in Nicaragua

Well before the Somoza regime fell, the Sandinista National Liberation Front (FSLN) committed itself to a mixed economy. The implicit role for the private sector had its origin in the FSLN's strategy of building alliances with all anti-Somoza actors during the revolutionary struggle. The FSLN itself was never strong enough politically or militarily to overthrow the Somoza regime. The large segment of the economic elite that was decidedly anti-Somoza had an important role in the revolution: it was not only significant in its own right but added domestic and international legitimacy to the revolution. The Sandinistas' commitment to a mixed economy helped win the allegiance of the anti-Somoza economic elite by allaying fears that the death of Somoza meant their death as well. All those who participated in ousting the dictator would enjoy legitimacy in the new Nicaragua. "National unity" became both a slogan and a mandate.

The political basis for a mixed economy was reinforced by the technical and administrative inability of the Sandinistas to assume complete responsibility for Nicaragua's economy. There were two obstacles to such an extreme result. First, certain sectors of the economy, such as cotton production and individual enterprises, the Exxon oil refinery for example, demanded technical and management skills that the Sandinistas did not have. Equally daunting, the sheer number of individuals and enterprises in other sectors of the economy, particularly in the production and distribution of foodstuffs, made complete nationalization of the economy unthinkable. The Sandinista leaders were aware of their dependence and the extent to which it constrained their autonomy. Those within Sandinista ranks and outside who pushed for complete nationalization of the economy were dismissed as "ultraleft adventurists."

Thus, the FSLN was resigned to building a new Nicaragua with the participation of the erstwhile private sector. Attempting to do otherwise would have been political and economic suicide. Complete nationalization would have alienated the entire economic elite, giving it a unity, a mission, and a sense of urgency otherwise absent. It would likewise have alienated small- and medium-sized producers and tempted them to form an alliance with the economic elite against the FSLN. The Sandinistas' access to foreign assistance from a wide range of countries and multilateral agencies would have been problematic, if not impossible. Finally, the task of running the economy, single-handed, amidst the hostility of those whose assets had been expropriated, would have been overwhelming.

The participation of private enterprise was to be restricted, however. The FSLN used its authority to ensure that the activities of the private sector would contribute to the Sandinistas' conception of how Nicaragua was to be remade. The textbook used to orient politically Nicaragua's university students summarized this prescript in a comparison:

> There is an enormous difference between a "mixed economy" where the state is at the service of the capitalists and another "mixed economy" where the state limits the extraction of surplus value that the bourgeoisie obtain and channels the gains toward the most needy sectors. In the first case we find the "neo-capitalist" economies or, more appropriately, "state monopoly capitalism." In the second case we have our economic system.[1]

1. National Autonomous University of Nicaragua (UNAN), Department of Social Sciences, *Curso sobre la problemática actual* (Managua: UNAN, 1980), p. 14.

A less theoretical interpretation of the role of private entrepreneurs and managers was offered by Commander Jaime Wheelock, a member of the FSLN's National Directorate:

> Their place in the revolution has been that of those who are called upon to prepare the food at a banquet. They are not invited to the banquet. They are only the ones who prepare the food. And we want to keep them hidden away in the kitchen, not to come out.[2]

The proffered justification for the control of the private sector is both the urgency of Nicaragua's poverty and the erstwhile elite's usurpation—and at times waste—of the nation's income.

The first proclamation of the newly constituted government, issued a month before its triumph, committed the regime to a mixed economy but made no reference to either its complexity or inherent tensions.[3] Shortly later, an internal FSLN party document discussed at length the contradictions in the envisioned mixed economy and the dangers the strategy posed to the Sandinistas' desired hegemony.[4] Tensions did, in fact, quickly emerge between "national unity" and control of private enterprise. Conflict crested in late 1981 with an open letter from the Superior Council of Private Enterprise (COSEP) and the ensuing jailing of COSEP leaders. More consequential—and more enduring—has been the quiet and often hidden struggle over resources. This prosaic struggle has involved the whole gamut of independent economic actors, from peasants to petty traders to well-endowed landowners.[5]

As significant as the private sector's participation and cooperation have been to postrevolutionary Nicaragua, the Sandinistas perceived the economic harbinger of progress to be the newly

2. James Austin and John Ickis, "Management, Managers, and Revolution," World Development 14 (1986): 785.

3. Encuentro, no. 17, n.d., pp. 31–47.

4. National Directorate of the Sandinista National Liberation Front (FSLN), "Análisis de la coyuntura y tareas de la revolución popular sandinista" (Managua, 1979, Mimeographed).

5. Discussed in Forrest D. Colburn, Post-Revolutionary Nicaragua (Berkeley: University of California Press, 1986).

constituted state sector, which would figure in its solution to the nation's serious problems:

> the Government of National Reconstruction, as its first measure, would proceed to recuperate all of the assets the Somoza family and its accomplices accumulated through extortion and rape.[6]

The Government of National Reconstruction did promptly expropriate Somoza's wealth and designate it national patrimony, to be managed by the state. This patrimony, named the Area of the People's Property, APP, was held to be the "axis of reactivation and reconstruction."[7] "The earnings generated by the Area of the People's Property will serve to finance savings and social expenditures."[8] It was to be the "future base of the people's power."[9] The very size of the APP made it important, but it came to have even greater significance because (1) it was managed by "revolutionaries"; (2) it was to receive preferential access to the nationalized financial system and other government organs; (3) linked to the second point, it was to be the site of state-initiated investment; (4) it provided an alternative to problematic private enterprises; and (5) it was perceived by many Nicaraguans, rightly or wrongly, as the potential sole economic actor in the distant future, when Nicaragua had made a gradual transition to socialism. Literally and figuratively, much was invested in the APP and—less explicitly but no less significantly—in the state's capacity to manage it.

As a Soviet scholar has noted, the swift establishment of the APP was not only economically significant but politically fortuitous, especially contrasted to the formation of the public sector in Cuba. The extensive property of Somoza was almost universally held to be little more than stolen property, rightfully to be expropriated. In other words, it was already public. Nationaliza-

6. *Encuentro*, no. 17, n.d., p. 31.
7. Ministry of Planning (MIPLAN), *Programa económico de austeridad y eficiencia 81* (Managua: MIPLAN, 1981), p. 158.
8. UNAN, *Curso*, p. 17.
9. From a speech by Commander Jaime Wheelock, quoted in Lucrecia Lozano, "Los albores de la revolución," in *Centroamérica: Una historia sin retoque*, ed. Instituto de investigaciones económicas, UNAM (Mexico City: El Día en Libros, 1987), p. 252.

tion of nearly one quarter of the economy alienated no one—no powerful foreign interests or national bourgeoisie. Thus, the Sandinistas acquired control of the economy "sufficient" for beginning with a "minimum of traumas."[10]

Although the Nicaraguan Revolution, in the words of this Soviet scholar, had good "objective possibilities" for beginning "transformations," the Sandinista leadership never stated its intended objectives with any specificity and how it would address the formidable problems facing Nicaragua. Yet the state was assuming direction of the economy, and the leadership had choices to make, especially in the APP where the state had nearly complete autonomy. Its pronouncements only suggested that economic recovery was to be pursued in an effort to improve the welfare and earning power of the poor. Aside from assigning priority to the state, it said little about the country's development strategy other than that emphasis on agriculture would continue, with a desire for heightened modernization of the sector and a gradual increment in the processing of agricultural commodities (especially those destined for export). Trade was to be diversified, but not for specific economic reasons.

What existed at the onset of postrevolutionary rule was more a political and economic mentalité than a structured set of policy guidelines. The mentalité opposed Somoza, oligarchies, and imperialists; it was suspicious of private initiative, markets, and capitalist institutions and sympathetic to the poor, state initiative, socialist countries, and socialist ideology. Equally important, though, is what the mentalité did not contain: intervals or scales that would give relative weights for its different values and beliefs. Accordingly, on many issues where decisions needed to be made, only predilections could be deduced. And on certain issues, such as the omnipresent trade-off between the rates of national consumption and national saving, it offered no clue as to how decisions should be made.

In part the Sandinista leadership's use of a collective mentalité to guide decision making came from the novelty of governing. Probably more important was the daunting—and dangerous—

10. Kiva Maydanik, "La unidad: Un problema clave," in *La revolución en Nicaragua*, ed. Alexandr Sujostat (Moscow: Editorial Progreso, 1985), p. 109.

environment in which decisions were to be made. Economic loss, damage, and disruption from the insurrection were considerable. The coffers of the treasury were empty, yet there was a high per capita foreign debt. Nicaragua's neighbors and the United States viewed the revolution with trepidation. Within the country, at least parts of the private sector and the church hierarchy were jittery. The poor held expectations for relief from the exigencies of poverty. In brief, resources were scarce and unpredictable, whereas demands (and fears) were abundant.

In such a vexatious environment, decisions are made not in a vacuum but in response to pressure. And in a poor country devastated by an insurrection, whose victorious elite is committed to radical change, economics and politics fuse. No political decision can be made without thought of its economic cost. But more significant for revolutionaries intent on consolidating their political power, no economic decision can be made without consideration of its political costs and benefits.

For this set of reasons, the nationalization of Nicaragua's "commanding heights" began with considerable expectation and equal uncertainty, unheralded as the latter was. Tracing out the establishment, organization, ensuing reorganizations, and, above all, performance of the commanding heights provides a framework to understand how and why decisions were made, and with what effect in transforming Nicaragua.

## Expanding the Public Sector

Before 1979 the Nicaraguan state had a limited role. It did not participate in the production of goods and services. Its social services such as health and education were incomplete, both in percentage of population covered (with a pronounced urban bias) and quality of service; financial services were likewise limited. Such government entities as did exist had been formed either in the 1960s or the 1970s. Even the Central Bank was established only in 1960.[11]

11. Central American Institute of Public Administration (ICAP), "Las empresas públicas y otros organismos descentralizados en la república de Nicaragua" (San Jose, 1978, Mimeographed), p. 5.

On the eve of the revolution, the country had only nineteen public entities. Six of them were financial, including the Central Bank and a group of development banks (with one oriented to serve the peasantry). Another six entities were "national institutes," with a mandate to spur development—of commerce, of agriculture, and the like. There was a social security institute. Finally, seven state enterprises provided water, electricity, port services, rail transportation, and telephone and mail service. The total state sector (including the central government) accounted for only about 15 percent of Nicaragua's gross domestic product.[12]

There would have been an even more restricted state role had it not been for pressure exerted by foreign donors (principally the United States). At times these donors made the establishment of public entities a precondition for foreign assistance, a linkage begun in aid from the United States' Alliance for Progress. The state's activity increased after the devastating earthquake in 1972 that destroyed Managua.

The limited role of the state followed from a strategy for development that held that private initiative best contributed to progress, from concerns about the cost of government, from pronounced class divisions (which strengthened the elite's self-serving belief in the primacy of private property and initiative), and finally from the elite's indifference to the poor majority (an example of which is Somoza's alleged reply to requests that he increase funds for education, "If everyone is educated, who will pick the coffee?").

Economic interests and the prevailing mentalité not only restricted the formation of government entities, including that of state enterprises, but influenced how those already constituted were to be administered. In short, they were to deviate only minimally from the management of private enterprises. By law the public entities were

to be governed by a directorate composed of at least three members;

not to engage in activities other than those they are legally

12. David Ruccio, "The State and Planning in Nicaragua," in *The Political Economy of Revolutionary Nicaragua,* ed. Rose Spalding (Boston: Allen and Unwin, 1987), p. 64.

assigned, or to obtain financing from other than mandated channels;

to publish in the Official Register, periodically, accounting statements that clearly present their financial status;

to provide an annual accounting to the executive branch; and

to have a representative of the minority (opposition) party on the directorate.[13]

Some public entities were allowed—and expected—to receive government subsidy, and all had to have their operation and investment budgets approved by the executive branch (handled by a ministry) and then submit records of their year's activities for audit and evaluation.[14]

After World War II Nicaragua's private economy grew dramatically, at an average rate that was not only substantially higher than the population's rate of growth but also higher than that of other economies in Latin America. Its growth was interrupted in 1972 by a less favorable world economy and the earthquake, but Nicaragua's economy remained dynamic, though growth accentuated its deep inequalities. A 1975 study concluded that in the critical agricultural sector, employers accounted for only 3.5 percent of the economically active population yet received 63 percent of the gross income.[15] The weakness of the state allowed it to make only a minimal attempt at redirecting growth or redistributing wealth and income. Heightened economic inequalities, and the government's indifference to them, undoubtedly contributed in the late 1970s to a widespread desire for revolutionary change.

The triumph of the FSLN in ousting Somoza and in subsequently consolidating power expanded the state's authority and responsibilities. Existing programs and activities were broadened, most significantly in health and education. Wages, working conditions, and employer-worker relations received attention from a number of government organs. Defense spending in-

13. ICAP, "Las empresas públicas," p. 2.
14. Ibid., pp. 27–28.
15. Philip Warnken, *The Agricultural Development of Nicaragua* (Columbia: University of Missouri Press, 1975), p. 44.

creased substantially. Minor examples of enhanced state activity abounded.

Perhaps more significant, the state extended its activity into areas previously dominated by private enterprise. One was the economic "service" sector, a cluster of activities that facilitate or complement production. Banking, insurance, and foreign trade were nationalized. State corporations were established to administer the financial system. Foreign trade became the responsibility of a newly established ministry, the Ministry of Foreign Trade (MICE), and of six exporting enterprises. The state also assumed some responsibility for domestic commerce, through another new ministry, the Ministry of Internal Commerce (MICOIN). A separate agency, the Nicaraguan Enterprise for Basic Food Products (ENABAS), assumed increasing responsibility for the purchase, storage, transportation, and distribution of basic foodstuffs.

Governmental dominance of the service sector, coupled with traditional monetary and fiscal prerogatives, enabled the state— intentionally or not—to manipulate the fortunes and behavior of specific groups and, more generally, of classes. But results depended on the cooperation or at least acquiescence of private actors; the state could offer incentives and threats but did not alone determine outcomes. The widespread nationalization of land and capital, however, engaged the revolutionary regime in production and demonstrated the potential of the state—and of the revolution it represented.

The extension of the state into Nicaragua's economy is visible in every sector (Table 1). The changes in percentage are significant. But the biggest change is undoubtedly in the sector with the lowest percentage increment: agriculture. Measured in any of the conventional indices—contribution to the GDP, provision of employment, and generation of export earning—agriculture is the mainstay of Nicaragua. What the state does in agriculture is most visible and consequential.

## The People's Property

Nationalized property became the Area of People's Property (APP). Outside of the agrarian sector, the seized entities were

Table 1    State Participation in the Economy

|  | 1978 | | 1980 | |
|---|---|---|---|---|
|  | Public (%) | Private (%) | Public (%) | Private (%) |
| Agriculture | — | 100 | 21 | 79 |
| Manufacturing | — | 100 | 33 | 67 |
| Construction | 40 | 60 | 70 | 30 |
| Mining | — | 100 | 95 | 5 |
| Services[a] | 31 | 69 | 55 | 45 |
| Gross domestic product | 15 | 85 | 41 | 59 |

SOURCE: Ministry of Planning (MIPLAN).
[a]Services include banking, insurance, domestic and international commerce, transportation, and electricity.

eclectic: a few industrial plants of some importance, producing simple consumer goods like soap; an ice cream parlor; a disco-theque; and a hotel that rents beds by the hour. Their diversity creates managerial difficulties for the Ministry of Industry, which administers them. Of greater economic significance are a handful of national gold mines; though small and backward in technology, they generate some foreign exchange. (They are managed by an autonomous entity.) The collective economic weight of these enterprises, however, pales before that of the agricultural enterprises nationalized, principally because of Nicaragua's incipient industrialization.

The decree nationalizing the assets of Somoza and the *somocistas* endowed the APP with about 850,000 hectares of farmland. Initially, the confiscated property was thought to be half of the country's farmland, but it later proved to be closer to one-fourth. Still, it was not only vast but encompassed most of Nicaragua's agroindustrial complexes and about half of the country's large estates. It included hundreds of small farms, many formerly owned by members of the National Guard. In total, an estimated two thousand agrarian enterprises were nationalized. In the cultivation of the country's principal crops during 1981–1982 (Table 2), the state had a significant share except for the two crops produced almost exclusively by peasants, maize and beans. And

Table 2    State Participation in Agricultural
Production, 1981–1982 Agricultural Season

|  | Public (%) | Private (%) |
|---|---|---|
| Cotton | 21 | 79 |
| Coffee | 15 | 85 |
| Sugar | 45 | 55 |
| Meat | 15 | 85 |
| Rice | 56 | 44 |
| Maize | 9 | 91 |
| Beans | 3 | 97 |

SOURCE: Ministry of Agricultural Development and
Agrarian Reform (MIDINRA).

in the processing of agricultural commodities, state participation
has been even higher. For example, the state owns all of the
country's slaughterhouses.

The first decision regarding confiscated estates was simply to
keep them intact, not to parcel them out to landless or near-
landless peasants. One of the slogans of the insurrection had
been "land to the peasants," and many peasants expected to
receive plots from seized estates. Distribution of land to peasants
was forthcoming but only after two years had passed, and then
from land of marginal use to the APP or lately confiscated from
the private sector. The government preferred to explain that state
ownership and management were to maintain established levels
of mechanization and economies of scale and to continue production of export commodities. A confidant of one of the Sandinista
commanders asserted, though, that "the state decided to keep the
land for political purposes. Consolidation of power would be
based on the [Sandinista] army and control of the economy."[16]
Evaluating this political explanation is difficult, but it is plausible
and complements the expressed economic rationale.

Once the new government had decided to retain ownership of
the nationalized land and capital, it faced the task of administer-

16. He spoke on the condition of anonymity, June 1985.

ing its far-flung endowment. Barely a week after the Sandinistas marched into Managua, the Nicaraguan Institute for Agrarian Reform (INRA) was established to consolidate state agricultural enterprises, revive production, and formulate the country's agrarian reform. The institute was headed by Commander Jaime Wheelock, the most theoretically trained and accomplished of the nine Sandinistas who form the National Directorate of the FSLN. In contrast to the staff in the Ministry of Agriculture, the key personnel in INRA were all Sandinista cadres.

A centralized organization was hastily created in which INRA's property was grouped into three portfolios: agroindustries, state production units (UPEs), and service units.[17] The agroindustry portfolio included sugar mills, cotton gins, slaughterhouses, poultry farms, rice farms and mills, tobacco farms, and tobacco-, coffee-, and food-processing plants. These enterprises were designated Agroindustries of the Agrarian Reform (AGROINRA) and received attention and credit apart from other INRA enterprises. The director of each AGROINRA enterprise reported directly to the central office in Managua.

Production units were far more numerous but usually had less individual importance than AGROINRA's enterprises. For the most part, UPEs were either farms growing export crops or cattle ranches. By early 1980 there were 2,862 UPEs scattered all over the country (constituted from both nationalized and abandoned property). These enterprises were organized within INRA according to their principal activity, usually the cultivation of a crop destined for export. Given the number of UPEs, it was necessary to consolidate them. Firms engaged in similar activities and proximate to one another were organized into *complejos* (a good translation does not exist; the best would be "complexes"). The complejos were supervised by the INRA offices set up in each of Nicaragua's sixteen departments. These offices in turn reported to INRA's central office in Managua. In effect, the complejos

17. This discussion of the establishment of the agrarian APP draws heavily on Walter Krueger and James Austin, *Organization and Control of Agricultural State-Owned Enterprises: The Case of Nicaragua*, Working paper no. 19, Graduate School of Business Administration, Harvard University (Cambridge, Mass.: Harvard University Press, 1983), pp. 8–42.

were "offices" or "branches" of a ministry. They were not legally incorporated and independent state-owned enterprises.

The third group of INRA's enterprises were businesses that sold agricultural inputs and services: fertilizer plants, pesticide plants, suppliers of veterinary products, aerial crop-dusting service, land preparation, radio communications, retail suppliers of agricultural machinery and parts, and a national distributor of farm equipment. The directors of these enterprises, many of which were pieced together, reported directly to INRA's central office.

Like enterprises in the private sector, INRA's and AGRO-INRA's productive entities were sorely in need of credit after the disruptions engendered by the insurrection. The government ordered the nationalized financial system (SFN) to respond to credit needs. Credits to the agrarian APP were channeled through two centralized funds, one for AGROINRA and one for INRA at large. These accounts were intended as mechanisms of control, since the individual state enterprises were not legal entities, and bank administrators were reluctant to lend money directly to them. So production units presented their monthly cash needs to AGROINRA or INRA, which consolidated and requested them from the bank. The bank transferred the funds to AGROINRA and INRA, which disbursed them. The bank was to be repaid directly from the sales income of the production units, to be deposited in a special account.

The agrarian APP's initial organization and infusion of credit from the nationalized banking system were successful in reviving production. But problems quickly emerged. Aside from day-to-day administrative hurdles, the APP's centralized organization concentrated its decisions in Managua, where their sheer volume clogged channels and slowed activity. Once decisions were made in Managua, the central office had little clue as to how they were implemented. Concomitantly, it had no control or information about the ultimate destination of funds entrusted to productive entities. These two problems were brought to a head by a third problem: at the conclusion of the first agricultural season, AGROINRA's and INRA's enterprises repaid much less than half of the credit they had been extended by the bank. Some funds had been lent for investments; a few enterprises were suspected of retaining revenues for working capital. And some losses could be forgiven because of the often Herculean task of reorganizing and reviving production following the revolution. But those in Managua were uneasy about not knowing what was happening in the countryside, and about having inadequate control over it. Jittery bankers increased their apprehension.

In November 1980 (fifteen months after its establishment), INRA undertook a fundamental restructuring aimed at decentralization. Its measures included merging the Ministry of Agriculture with INRA, redefining the central office's responsibilities, consolidating departmental offices, disbanding AGROINRA, creating legal state enterprises out of the APP's productive entities, and designing a system of controls. First, INRA absorbed the old Ministry of Agriculture, which had ceased to have authority or responsibilities. It formed the Ministry of Agricultural Development and Agrarian Reform (MIDINRA). To define responsibilities more clearly and to spread the burden of decision making, it set up five vice-ministries: Economics, Agrarian Reform, Export Production, Livestock Production, and Basic Staples. No longer a separate entity, AGROINRA was included in the portfolio of the export vice-ministry. And the sixteen departmental INRA offices were reorganized into seven MIDINRA regions, using geographical and economic criteria. Finally, skilled personnel from the central offices in Managua were reassigned to the regions. The intention guiding these changes was to move authority and responsibility closer to centers of production.

A different kind of reform was the Agrarian Reform Enterprise Law, redefining the agricultural enterprises as legally constituted state enterprises. The law was published in the country's official register in December 1980 and MIDINRA subsequently implemented its basic tenets. The Agrarian Reform Enterprise Law and its stipulations clarified the duties and authority of the enterprises' directors, and even the relations among the enterprises, MIDINRA's regional offices, and MIDINRA Central.[18] It was postrevolutionary Nicaragua's first legislation of state enter-

18. Ministry of Agricultural Development and Agrarian Reform (MIDINRA), "Gestión de empresas de reforma agraria" (Managua, 1984, Mimeographed), appendix.

prises and inspired similar legislation for enterprises in the industrial sector.

The Agrarian Reform Enterprise Law established fifty-six production enterprises by amalgamating the complejos and UPEs. The new firms were huge—some spread over more than one department, embracing tens of thousands of hectares, and employing thousands of workers. And though the intent had been to group UPEs dedicated to similar activities, invariably there were queer inclusions. For example, the Enterprise Ramón Raudales was formed out of twenty-six UPEs, twenty-five of which were cattle ranches; the odd one had six hundred goats, which no one knew what to do with (Nicaraguans are not accustomed to eating goat's meat or dairy products).[19]

The fifty-six production units were complemented by the formation of ten agricultural service enterprises. The number of enterprises grew in the next few years, reaching 76 in 1982, and attaining a certain stability in 1984 with 101 enterprises: 38 agricultural, 30 agroindustrial, and 33 providing services to the country's agricultural sector at large.[20] Most of the growth has come from splitting up existing enterprises rather than adding new property to the APP.

With the Agrarian Enterprise Law in effect by February 1981, state agrarian enterprises gained significant authority and operating independence. In principle, the enterprises were freed from many cumbersome bureaucratic procedures that had stymied activity. Decisions about personnel, material, logistics, and credit came within the enterprises' jurisdiction. Equally important, the enterprises' legal status allowed the director to engage in credit transactions with the bank. This discretion enhanced financial flexibility.

These reforms did not affect Commander Wheelock's authority to appoint regional directors and the directors of individual enterprises; his political power and leadership have been considerable. MIDINRA Central exercises its influence through

19. Interview with César Gomez, accounting manager, the Enterprise Ramón Raudales, Managua, August 1985.

20. Lozano, "Los albores," p. 259; MIDINRA, "Directorio" (Managua, 1984, Mimeographed), p. 1.

planning—suggesting guidelines and allocating fungible resources (many from abroad); it also determines the disposal of any profit. MIDINRA Central's instructions to enterprises are sent through MIDINRA's regional offices, and its regional directors meet monthly with enterprise directors to evaluate the enterprises' projects and performance. (Regional directors ordinarily meet twice a month with the minister.)

The final component of the reform of the agrarian APP was the design and implementation of systems for planning and control. The perceived need for this capability anteceded the Agrarian Reform Enterprise Law, which shifted financial responsibilities to the enterprises. A control system in particular was required for the ministry, and the government of which it is a part, to ensure adherence to its aspirations and specific policies. Because the capacity to design systems for agricultural planning and control was limited in Nicaragua, Commander Wheelock asked the Cuban government to send two specialists in control systems. The Cubans designed a general control framework, the Uniform Administrative Control System (SUCA), composed of ten subsystems: planning, statistics, general and cost accounting, inventory, warehouse, fixed assets, organization, personnel, and auditing. The Cubans concentrated on accounting while MIDINRA's planning department was responsible for the planning and statistical systems.

An accounting system was designed but its implementation has been problematic and incomplete. First, it was overdesigned, excessively sophisticated for the complejos and UPEs, and often even for the central office of the enterprises. (It may be too complex for MIDINRA Central to digest all the data it is supposed to generate.) For each enterprise, a plethora of statements must be prepared: one daily, six monthly, sixteen quarterly, and one annually.[21] And these statements can be prepared only on the basis of information collected on a multitude of forms. Second, with some support from within MIDINRA Central, the Cubans changed the names and order of traditional accounting terminology. Current Assets, for example, was changed to Rotating Re-

21. MIDINRA, "Sistema de contabilidad de empresa" (Managua, n.d., Mimeographed).

sources and placed after, not before, Fixed Assets (or in the new lexicon, Basic Resources). Capital was renamed Patrimony of the People.[22] The changes engendered confusion, especially among those with training in traditional accounting. Third, training seminars did not reach all those who needed the training. Still, the accounting system does in principle provide a uniform record-keeping system. As one accountant at an enterprise put it, the system is useful if one "cuts steps."[23]

The original intention was that the accounting system would be implemented with a planning and, of lesser importance, a statistical system. Because of the enormity of the task and intraorganizational conflicts, an effective planning system was never designed, let alone integrated into the desired overall enterprise system. According to one MIDINRA official, success was limited to "planning the accounting."[24] To achieve goals other than "everyday" management of its enterprises, MIDINRA has only the setting of guidelines and the channeling of fungible resources. And, equally important, MIDINRA Central has no ability to evaluate its diverse and scattered enterprises: even if the elaborate control system were fully and effectively implemented, MIDINRA has no criteria to judge the success of the enterprises and to apply rewards or sanctions.

The newly constituted agrarian enterprises have considerable autonomy. The lack of effective planning and control systems has meant that directors receive so much latitude to do their "work" that by default they are the ones who decide just what their work is. MIDINRA Central makes many requests for information, but an enterprise must unfailingly produce only one document—the annual technical economic plan, a projection of the firm's annual activities in both physical and financial terms. The director uses information from the plan to receive credit from the bank. With money in hand, administrators do their best to meet the firm's

22. The nomenclature is the same used in Cuba. See Central Junta of Planning, *El sistema de dirección y planificación de la economía en las empresas* (Havana: Editorial de Ciencias Sociales, 1981), pp. 57–70.

23. Interview with Danilo Sánchez, accounting manager, the Enterprise Ricardo Morales, Chinandega, January 1985.

24. Interview with Mario Alemán, administrator, MIDINRA Central, Managua, January 1985.

objectives and to keep accounts of what they do. They need not fear audit or evaluation.

## Economic Troubles and Political Survival

Exactly what the Sandinista regime wants from its state enterprises has never been made explicit. Perhaps the clearest, and most accurate, statement comes from an internal MIDINRA document worth quoting at length:

> With the consolidation of the agrarian APP, the revolutionary state has attempted to establish the bases for a new economy (new relations of strength, new social relations, and work in the countryside) and hence has defined as priority objectives in the APP sector:
>
> 1. create autonomous sources of accumulation to diminish the dependence of the country on international capital;
> 2. develop new forms of production and of workers' participation;
> 3. substantially improve living and working conditions of agricultural laborers;
> 4. demonstrate the economic advantages of large-scale state production and centralized planning;
> 5. form entities to assist the production and commercialization of small [peasant] production and show the advantages of integration into superior forms of organization;
> 6. try to resolve the "productive backwardness" of peasants through the provision of technical assistance, credit, and state commercialization.[25]

This list of goals is far ranging and ambitious. But there is no set priority that could guide decision making of those actually administering the agrarian APP. This ambiguity is evident outside of Managua. A representative view was expressed by two administrators in the office of MIDINRA's fourth region (in Estelí):

25. MIDINRA, "La política para el APP" (Managua, 1982, Mimeographed), p. 1.

"The enterprises have many objectives. Planning is done with a notion to develop the region."[26]

Despite the multitude of aspirations for the agrarian APP, only the failure of the first goal on this list—capital accumulation—has repeatedly brought the agrarian APP to the attention of the Sandinista regime at large. The APP's inability to monitor or evaluate in detail its individual enterprises limits information on their success in meeting other objectives. But the bank's financial statements provide regular aggregate, or macro-, information about the APP's financial performance. First public mention of the problem of the APP's financial losses was obliquely buried in the *Programa económico de austeridad y eficiencia 81,* a statement of what the government had accomplished in its first full year of service and planned for the coming year. "The lack of financial discipline in the APP" was held partly responsible for "the lack of internal saving," compensated by foreign credit and an increase in the money supply.[27] The latter was acknowledged to be inflationary. Elsewhere, though, the program held that "in the future, it is anticipated that the voluntary saving of the people and the profits of the APP will progressively substitute . . . foreign loans and monetary emissions."[28] (Monetary emissions are the printing of currency.)

The losses of the APP continued and even increased, prompting a pointed assessment in an internal MIDINRA report, written in 1982:

> . . . Problems have impeded the attainment of the objectives of the enterprises, generating profits and creating a source of accumulation. . . . If they do not increase their efficiency, the maintenance of these enterprises can be done only by:
>
> a state subsidy (financed by whom?) as would be the case if prices for agroexport commodities were increased without a corresponding increase in international prices;
>
> an increase in the prices of commodities for the domestic market;

---

26. Interview with Manuel Castro and Fidel Olivas, administrators, office of MIDINRA's fourth region, Estelí, January 1985.
27. MIPLAN, *Programa económico*, p. 164.
28. Ibid., p. 137.

a combination of the two. The inflationary consequences of these policies are well known: the first solution equals an increase in earnings without an increase in goods produced (which results in an increase in demand, which leads to an increase in prices and imports); and the second solution raises the prices of basic consumer goods, raises social tensions, and increases wages and salaries that have repercussions for production costs (the beginning of the "price-wage spiral"). Neither of these policies can be solutions to the deficit problem of the enterprises of the APP.[29]

The questions implicit in the assessment proved to be enduring.

Public attention in Nicaragua to the APP's financial problems came with the first newspaper headlines on the enterprises' performance. The 7 March 1985 issue of *Barricada,* the newspaper of the FSLN, bore the headline, "Every State Enterprise Should Be Profitable." The newspaper, *El Nuevo Diario,* sympathetic to the FSLN, bore a similar headline. The accompanying articles reported on a speech by Commander Wheelock to four hundred directors of the APP's agrarian and industrial enterprises. He asserted:

> The state enterprises that this year do not show prospects of profitability will be closed, regardless of what they produce and where they are located. . . . We are going to end this policy of enterprises that are subsidized.[30]

Commander Wheelock's speech was prompted by the accelerated losses of the agrarian APP. The debt of the enterprises as of 30 June 1981 was 1.9 billion córdobas, representing 46 percent of the enterprises' capital. By 31 March 1984 the debt had risen to 8.8 billion córdobas, almost a fivefold increase in three years.[31] In the interval the real value of the córdoba, always difficult to measure because of governmental controls, had declined, but not nearly as rapidly as the APP's debt had increased. Another indicator of the enterprises' losses is that in the 1983–

29. MIDINRA, "La política para el APP," pp. 28–29.
30. *Barricada,* 7 March 1985; *El Nuevo Diario,* 7 March 1985. The text of the speech was printed in *Informaciones agropecuarias,* March–April 1985.
31. MIDINRA, "Problemática de las empresas del sector agropecuario adscritas al MIDINRA" (Managua, 1985, Mimeographed), table 13 in the appendix.

1984 agricultural season, only 30 percent of the credit extended was repaid.[32]

The losses of the agrarian APP have been general. In the first six years of postrevolutionary rule, only a handful of enterprises were profitable—two, three, or four in any given year. Among the others, the magnitude of their losses is explained by neither location nor activity. Enterprises in every business and in every part of the country lost money. Indeed, the most profitable firm and the one that consistently recorded the largest losses both grew the same crop—cotton.

Despite Commander Wheelock's admonition, no state enterprises were closed, continued losses notwithstanding. But MIDINRA Central accelerated its efforts to improve the management of the APP. In addition to improving the technical plan and enrolling key managers in seminars, the state has tried to cultivate a new mentalité, one that emphasizes efficiency, productivity, and profitability.

Efforts to improve the financial performance of the APP have been overwhelmed by a deterioration in the economic environment in which it does business. From the beginning, enterprises had a daunting environment: political tensions, shortages, a trade embargo imposed by the United States, counterrevolution, and an omnipresent uncertainty. In February 1985, though, the government announced a number of economic measures, including prominently the devaluation of the córdoba by 280 percent and the rescindment of a host of price controls. These measures helped accelerate inflation. According to the United Nations' Economic Commission for Latin America and the Caribbean (CEPAL), Nicaragua's rate of inflation in 1986 was 747 percent, the highest in Latin America that year.[33] In 1987 inflation rose to four-digit figures and the Nicaraguan government was forced to issue larger denominated currency. In early 1988, with inflation at an estimated annual rate of 7,000 percent, the government reissued currency at a rate of 1 to 1,000. But inflation only

32. MIDINRA, "Evaluación financiera de las empresas de reforma agraria, ciclo 1983–1984" (Managua, 1984, Mimeographed), p. 5.
33. Economic Commission for Latin America and the Caribbean (CEPAL), *La evolución de la economía de América Latina en 1986* (Santiago: CEPAL, 1988), p. 40.

accelerated, surpassing an annual rate of 20,000 percent in the final months of 1988.

The loss of price stability made evaluating the financial performance of the APP close to impossible. Most enterprises suddenly became "profitable" because their costs were at the beginning of the year and their revenues at the end. Depreciation became meaningless, as did payments of interest and principal. Enterprises that are most profitable are those that produce for internal demand or engage in commerce. But enterprises that produce export commodities seem less profitable only because state monopsonies have lagged in raising their prices. The combination of inflation and price distortions has made calculations of efficiency illusory.

As Nicaraguan economists have pointed out, the surge in inflation cannot be blamed on the reforms of February 1985 but must instead be traced to the accumulated imbalances between supply and demand.[34] The Sandinista regime has pursued expansionary fiscal and monetary policies without a corresponding increase in production. Indeed, the agroindustrial sector, which represents 75 percent of the entire industrial sector by the value of its output, has operated at less than 50 percent of capacity.[35] Correspondingly, the country's exports have fallen by about 50 percent since 1977 (the last year the government considers the economy "normal"). Adding to woes, the international prices of Nicaragua's export commodities have generally been weak in the post-revolutionary epoch.

The counterrevolution, with its multifaceted costs, has greatly aggravated the economic crisis. That the revolutionary state would be wracked by counterrevolution was apprehended by the FSLN, as was perhaps foot dragging in the private sector. From the beginning of their rule, the Sandinista leaders were aware of limits to their authority. What is surprising, though, is that even where the Sandinistas had considerable autonomy—prominently, in the APP—managerial limitations have made even the "state" a

34. For example, José Luis Medal, "Políticas de estabilización y ajuste estructural en Nicaragua (1980–1986)," (San Jose, 1987, Mimeographed).
35. See MIDINRA, *Marco prospectivo del desarrollo agro-industrial*, vols. 1–2 (Managua: MIDINRA, 1985).

serious problem for the FSLN. The nationalized commanding heights have not been the "axis for economic reactivation." Instead, they have had a deleterious effect on an already weak and beleaguered economy. The nationalized commanding heights have also been an administrative headache: for example, revising the price of sugar involves five ministries, requires President Daniel Ortega's approval, and takes six months.

For the Sandinista leadership, Nicaragua's economic problems are especially menacing because they influence popular support for the FSLN and its revolutionary program. And as Commander Wheelock pointed out when he addressed the gathering of enterprise directors mentioned earlier, support is conditioned not only by the general state of the economy but also by perceptions of the government's administrative capability. Wheelock warned, "It is important that we are conscious that our people . . . observe us, they observe the enterprise director, they observe wisely; our people know how we use resources."[36] In short, at stake with the APP is not just Nicaragua's economy but also the Sandinista regime's legitimacy.

Nonetheless, the obverse of the economic problems is the political survival of the FSLN. Despite protracted economic difficulties, civil opposition, and a counterrevolution generously supported by the United States, the Sandinista regime has survived the early—and engrossing—years of postrevolutionary rule. The Sandinistas have drawn on many resources to consolidate and maintain their power. Command of the economy has been one such resource. Most of the previously listed goals for the agrarian APP had a political dimension. And given the politically charged environment the enterprises work in, they cannot avoid having a political impact. They are outposts, or flags, of the revolution. But there are no macrolevel assessments of how the agrarian APP has responded to political aspirations and challenges. An understanding, and explanation, of how the nationalized commanding heights have figured in the successes and failures of the Sandinista regime can be gleaned by reviewing the decisions made in three representative state enterprises before Nicaragua's inflationary surge in late 1985.

36. *Informaciones agropecuarias*, March–April 1985.

# 3

## The Enterprise
## Oscar Turcios

Costs? Another department is looking after
that.
——Raúl Camas, manager of one of Oscar
Turcios's complejos

    The Cuban Revolution prompted some Cuban tobacco
growers to emigrate to Central America. A handful came to Nicaragua and settled in three areas of northwestern Nicaragua where
climate and soil especially suit the cultivation of cigar-leaf
tobacco—Estelí, Condega, and Jalapa. The start-up costs in tobacco cultivation are high, as are annual production costs, but
Somoza provided credit in exchange for a share in the business
associations the Cubans were encouraged to form. Somoza later
owned two farms outright. Tobacco had long been cultivated in
Nicaragua—perhaps before the Spanish conquest—but only inter-
mittently by small farmers for their consumption. Cuban talent,
Somoza money, and cheap labor in the economically depressed
region combined to make cultivation of tobacco lucrative. Production began in 1963 and quickly expanded. The high costs of production and extensive skills necessary to cultivate tobacco kept
others from planting tobacco, but the original group of cultivators
increased their volume of production as rapidly as they could. The
end of commercial relations between Cuba and the United States
gave Nicaraguan producers a ready market. Tobacco became the

principal source of employment and income in the region and made a small contribution to the national balance of payments.[1]

Because of their ties to Somoza, the Cuban tobacco growers had their estates in Nicaragua confiscated after the revolution in July 1979; Somoza's farms were also taken over. The Cubans went to Miami or to Honduras (the largest producer of tobacco in Central America). A newly formed governmental institute, the National Institute for Agrarian Reform (INRA), assumed responsibility for managing the tobacco farms. Although the farms were spread out in three disparate locations, INRA grouped them all into one enterprise, which it named after the revolutionary martyr Oscar Turcios. The Nicaraguan Cigar Company, owned in part by Somoza, had likewise been confiscated and included in Oscar Turcios. It was managed autonomously and eventually separated itself to become an independent enterprise (retaining its original name for marketing purposes).[2]

The single remaining private producer was a Cuban who had over the years resolutely refused to have anything to do with Somoza. Since he was a small producer, for all practical purposes the state assumed complete responsibility for the production of tobacco in Nicaragua after the triumph of the revolution.

## Founding of the Enterprise Oscar Turcios

The Oscar Turcios enterprise began with what was confiscated and little else. There were thirty-five farms, with six drying and curing centers. Total acreage was 3,361 manzanas, of which only 980 manzanas were planted in tobacco.[3] However, total land suitable for the cultivation of tobacco was estimated to be 2,083 manzanas. Compared with cotton or coffee estates, this acreage does not seem like a lot; but in tobacco it is, because the

---

1. Institute for National Development (INFONAC), *Posición competitiva del tabaco tipo habano producido en Nicaragua con respecto al mercado norteamericano* (Managua: INFONAC, 1967), pp. 38–45; INFONAC, *Programa trienal de desarrollo tabacalero* (Managua: INFONAC, 1966), pp. 5–6.

2. Center for the Study of Agrarian Reform (CIERA), *Lunes socioeconómico de Barricada* (Managua: MIDINRA, 1984), pp. 94–98.

3. One manzana (mz) = 0.7 hectares, or 1.7 acres.

extensive labor requirements per manzana far exceed those for cotton or coffee. Land was divided between Jalapa, with 2,260 manzanas fit for tobacco but only 741 manzanas actually under cultivation, and Estelí, with 823 manzanas suitable for cultivation and 239 under cultivation. Roughly 60 percent of production was in Jalapa with the balance in Estelí.[4] The enterprise had machinery and a stock of necessary supplies but next to no working capital.

The firm began amid chaos and confusion. Managers were appointed by INRA to replace the departed Cubans, but they were often inexperienced and unsure of their responsibilities. What saved the enterprise was the permanence of many field hands, supervisors, and agricultural technicians, some of whom had ten to twenty years of experience growing tobacco. These workers knew roughly what needed to be done and carried on their work, though not always as efficiently as might have been hoped. The newly nationalized banking system provided necessary working capital.

The workers proudly held the enterprise to be part of the Property of the People (APP); but nobody ever explained the implications of that term for managing the enterprise. What were the objectives of the enterprise? to help develop the region? to facilitate the transformation of the economy? to provide employment to those without employment? to earn a profit for the state? By what criteria would the enterprise and its administration be judged? Or would the enterprise and its administration be judged at all? Before the revolution, the objective had been to produce a profit through cultivating tobacco. Fulfilling that objective necessitated production but also control of quality (to ensure high revenues) and of costs. With the difficulty of simply maintaining output after the revolution, and in the absence of any clearly defined goal for the enterprise, the motto of the enterprise became "to produce at whatever cost." The volume of production became more important than the difference between costs and revenues.

Just maintaining historic levels of production has been diffi-

4. Ministry of Agricultural Development and Agrarian Reform (MIDINRA), "Directorio" (Managua, 1984, Mimeographed).

cult for the enterprise. Initial chaos followed the abrupt transfer of private farms to a single state enterprise under new management. With time, order was restored, at least for the most part. However, new problems arose—principally with labor and shortage of inputs. Thus, maintaining the rhythm of production was still a challenge or, as one administrator put it, "a headache."[5]

By 1983 MIDINRA Central realized that the geographic dispersion of the enterprise was too taxing. It transferred the eighteen farms (UPEs) located in Jalapa from Oscar Turcios to another firm, the Enterprise Laureano Mairena. The division also took into account strategic reasons: Jalapa is on the border with Honduras and thus has suffered attacks from counterrevolutionaries based in Honduras. For reasons that the state never made clear to the administrators at Oscar Turcios, the new firm began without the debts that corresponded to the farms in Jalapa. Oscar Turcios was left with the debt.

The Oscar Turcios enterprise never really assumed management of the few farms in the third tobacco region, Condega. This land became a special project that the Bulgarian government has undertaken with the ambitious goal of planting ten thousand manzanas of light tobacco (for cigarettes) over six years. It seems doubtful that the project will reach this lofty goal, but the scale of the project and its high salaries attracted many agricultural workers and technicians away from Oscar Turcios. Thus, the reorganization of Oscar Turcios left it responsible only for the area of Estelí, freeing it from unwieldy managerial responsibilities in other zones. However, Oscar Turcios paid a price—one zone saddled the firm with debt and the other zone lured away many of its skilled personnel.[6]

## Growing Tobacco

In Nicaragua the production of dark-leaf tobacco for cigars is said to have three stages: cultivating, preindustrial, and industrial. Cultivation includes everything from the preparation

5. Interview with Hector Valdivia, director, February 1985.
6. Ibid.

of the soil to the transportation of harvested tobacco to drying barns. In the drying barns most of the preindustrial work takes place—the manual separation and preparation of individual leaves for drying as well as the drying itself. The preindustrial stage includes the packing of dried tobacco in wooden boxes and its shipment to the Nicaraguan Cigar Company. It also involves the trimming and curing of tobacco leaves. The so-called industrial process consists of women hand-rolling cigars with the aid of only knives and simple wooden presses.

Tobacco requires intensive care throughout its cultivation—planting, transplanting, pruning, maturation, and harvesting. The practice of cultivating cigar-leaf tobacco under artificial cheesecloth shade, which maintains a high moisture content in soil and air, requires heavy but careful irrigation from planting until the last harvest. But though tobacco is a labor intensive crop, the demand for labor fluctuates; it is greatest during planting and, above all, harvest. Seedlings are transplanted 45 days after their germination, and harvesting begins after another 180 days. Harvesting is carried out every 10 days; plants offer eight harvests.

Harvesting is carried out for the summer crop from October to June, and the winter crop is harvested from April to September. (In Nicaragua, winter falls during the rainy season, from May to October; summer stretches from November to April.) The two harvesting periods do not neatly coincide with the more common agricultural cycles in Nicaragua; consequently, the results of any given year's activities fall in different fiscal periods.

Harvesting concludes with the stringing together of leaves with needle and thread. The leaves, grouped like so many pearls on a necklace, are dried for a month. After the *zapadura,* or removal of the thread holding bunches of leaves together, leaves are classified and packaged. Bundles of leaves are cured in a cool warehouse for two months, a period essential in giving the tobacco its taste and aroma. Unless the tobacco is to be exported in bulk form, stems are then removed from leaves, and the crisp leaves are made ready for rolling into cigars.[7]

7. Interview with Freddy Valdiva, technician, February 1985.

## Labor

Obtaining high yields of the quality of tobacco that receives the best price requires extensive and careful work. Labor is the single most important and the costliest input. Unfortunately, however, labor presents the most serious problem at the Oscar Turcios enterprise. There is an acute shortage of labor, and in fact children and women do almost all of the work. They cannot accomplish as much as men, though they must be paid about the same wage. Equally important, this pool of labor is inexperienced. One of the firm's agricultural technicians estimated that before the revolution 80 percent of the labor force in any given year had experience working with tobacco. In 1985 only 15 percent of the labor force had any experience.[8]

Administrators of the UPEs speculate that there are three principal reasons why the firm has only a handful of able-bodied men. Many men in the region are in the military. The military occasionally visits the enterprise, looking for recruits; the first time this happened, workers ran away and never returned. Finally, wages at the enterprise are lower than those for other work in the area, especially construction.

Just as problematic as the shortage of labor is the productivity of the labor available. Since the revolution, labor productivity has fallen dramatically. At first, laborers rejected requests to maintain historic levels of productivity by saying, "*somos libres* (we are free)." Now their common retort is that salaries justify no more than a minimal effort. Workers respond to exhortations by saying, "You are too demanding; the salary is very low."[9] Laborers are not above working only two hours then leaving, claiming later (at payday) that they worked a full day. Also, a few laborers steal items such as small motors and irrigation pipes to sell in the private sector. For selfish gains, many workers have exploited the sympathy of the revolutionary government for their class. There is no established procedure for

8. Interview with Tomás Fuentes, manager of the administration center, February 1985.
9. Interview with Santo López, manager of a UPE, February 1985.

castigating unproductive workers, which makes it hard to rectify low productivity.[10]

The use of children, the majority of them between eight and fourteen years old, presents problems of its own. Children lack the physical capacity to do demanding manual labor and the discipline to work constantly. For many children, the firm is little more than a playground. As one director of a UPE exclaimed, "Here you have to be a papa, a schoolteacher, and everything else."[11]

Labor is also problematic because of the counterrevolution, which generates fear and uncertainty. The enterprise has not suffered from attack by counterrevolutionaries, but one young agricultural technician working for the enterprise maintained that there are two wars in Nicaragua—the actual war and the war of rumors. According to him, local people believe that "he who works for the state is a dead man." Within the enterprise laborers and workers are said to be fearful. Fear of retribution may explain in part why the firm finds it difficult to attract able-bodied men, though this explanation was not made by those discussing labor problems. The extent to which fear and uncertainty have contributed to lackluster labor productivity is impossible to measure but may be relevant. Another difficult question remains: to what extent does the danger of counterrevolutionary recruitment of the rural poor inhibit Oscar Turcios and other similarly situated state enterprises from pressing laborers to be more productive?

## Administration

For those managing the production of tobacco, labor problems are the principal grievance and absorb prodigious quantities of time. These problems can become ridiculous: one technician recalled a driver whose tractor was broken down for two or three months. He refused to do any other type of work, saying he was a tractor driver. In addition to labor problems, those directly in charge of production face another typical situation—the

10. Ibid.
11. Ibid.

chronic shortage of spare parts, nearly all of which are imported. Jeeps, tractors, irrigation pumps, the equipment for drying tobacco, all can be immobilized for the lack of a single part, necessitating considerable resourcefulness to solve the problem. Transportation is also a serious problem because of the lack of vehicles and shortages of gas.

These problems, and the efforts that administrators must make to cope with them, inevitably translate into high production costs. If purchases of parts have to be made on the black market, then costs will rise. If it takes two women to do the work that used to be done by a single man—and since women and men must receive the same wage—then labor costs will double. If the firm must pay for workers who are mobilized for defense, then labor costs will be higher. Likewise if work is less than satisfactory, yields and quality with fall, both of which will hurt revenues. If—as is the case—children harvesting the tobacco damage over 20 percent of the harvest, revenues inescapably fall.

While the enterprise confronts a series of problems that are not of its making but that nonetheless raise the cost of production, those supervising production make little effort to evaluate costs and to take necessary remedies. The manager of a complejo responded to a question about his efforts to control costs, "Costs? Another department is looking after that."[12] Those supervising production have an idea of how things should be done, but they have no idea about the details of production costs or how to obtain such information. The firm lacks controls in the warehouses, which are located in every UPE. All workers in the countryside—even managers of complejos and UPEs—have the attitude that their job is to grow and process tobacco. Exorbitant cost overruns are simply blamed on the problems that are outside the firm's control.

The complejo manager quoted earlier went so far as to state, "Production costs are not important because they are in córdobas." He outlined his analysis of the firm's financial problems:

> The problem of the firm's losses resides in the exchange rate. There is a lot of confusion over prices. The córdoba is not stable.

12. Interview with Raúl Camas, manager of a complejo, February 1985.

Last year the price paid by the state was equivalent to an exchange rate of 15.40 córdobas to the dollar. If it had been 30 córdobas, tobacco would have been profitable.[13]

With this attitude, there is not much incentive to control costs. Managers can blame high production costs on the shortage of labor, poor labor productivity, the shortage of spare parts, or other problems. Concomitantly, the firm can cover high production costs by simply asking the state to pay higher prices for tobacco. Since the exchange rate is set by the government and not by the market, everyone perceives that the government can change the prices it pays whenever and however it likes. If the Ministry of Agricultural Development and Agrarian Reform (MIDINRA) is not willing to pay a higher price, then the enterprise can ask the nationalized banking system to provide additional funding, offering the justification that state prices are inadequate.

The attitude of those in the fields toward a firm's administration reveals not only a separation between production and administration but also their lack of respect for administrators. As one of the firm's technicians complained, "There is programming, not planning."[14] Administrators do not consult with those in the countryside. According to the technician, this lack of participation resulted in great errors, entailing the misuse of resources. He maintained that the administration could not even provide needed information, an inadequacy that mystified him because the administration is large. He saw contradiction between the existence of an excessively staffed administration and its inability to adequately administer the firm. The technician maintained that the administration was simply a "white elephant" and that if he were the director of the enterprise he would "fire a lot of people."[15]

## Leadership

In the five years the enterprise has existed, it has had five directors. The present director acknowledges that the firm has

13. Ibid.
14. Interview with Félix Pedro Rivera, manager of production, February 1985.
15. Ibid.

serious problems. The firm loses money every year and has a staggering debt for which it cannot even pay the yearly interest charges. The director mourns, "We are not going to be prosperous."[16] He reports that presently there is no information on costs per complejo and no control over expenses.

The director feels compelled to spend most of his time out in the countryside and not at his desk. He immerses himself in problems that obstruct production, moving from crisis to crisis. He carries a little book containing important information he needs to administer and represent the firm. The data do not come from the departments of accounting, economics, planning, or personnel. Instead he himself gathers the data when he is in the countryside, at the bank, or whenever else he can. Given the urgent problems confronting the enterprise and the director's perceived need for personal attention to them, the director has little time to take a long-range view of the firm or its management. As he freely admits, "I don't know where I'm going."[17]

The administrative manager of the enterprise is of the opinion that the firm has suffered from disorganization. In his opinion there are three continuing problems: poor salaries have caused a high turnover of personnel; the management's responsibilities constantly change; and MIDINRA Central has not given the enterprise a structure.[18] The last explanation suggests that the firm lacks the ability or motivation to act on its own—to solve its own problems. Its administration is organized into departments, but the departments do not adequately coordinate their activities. For example, when the administrative manager was asked if he passed on documents to the firm's accountants, he replied, "No, accounting is another department."[19]

There are no evaluations of personnel in the administration. Evaluations would make little difference, however: since as long as anyone can remember, no one has been fired or severely reprimanded for poor performance. There is likewise no evaluation of departments or of the overall costs of the administration. Of those in charge of the different departments none are aware of the

16. Interview with Hector Valdivia, director, February 1985.
17. Ibid.
18. Interview with Diego López, manager of administration, February 1985.
19. Ibid.

*Table 3    Oscar Turcios: Monthly Costs of Administrative Personnel (in córdobas)*

| Sector | Activity | Personnel | Total Cost | Average Salary |
|--------|----------|-----------|------------|----------------|
| Tobacco | Agricultural | 163 | 674,200 | 4,110.97 |
| Tobacco | Preindustrial | 38 | 189,900 | 4,997.36 |
| Tobacco | Industrial | 109 | 778,400 | 7,141.28 |
| Basic grains | All stages | 25 | 117,200 | 5,088.00 |
| | | 335 | 1,759,700 | 5,266.96 |

SOURCE: Enterprise Oscar Turcios, Economics, February 1985.

monthly costs of their department. Perhaps even more troubling is the sentiment of the economic manager that administrative costs are fixed costs, implying that they are beyond reproach.[20]

Figures provided by the accounting department suggest that, in fact, administrative costs are exceedingly high (Table 3). There are approximately 3,000 workers involved in production compared to 336 in administration. Average monthly salaries are much higher for administrators than for those in production, thus raising the percentage of administrative costs to total costs.[21] Of course, the best measure of administrative costs is its relation to total costs. As can be calculated from the Oscar Turcios income statement (Table 4), the firm's administrative costs are 24 percent of total production costs, a figure that by any criterion is inordinately high.

## Accounting and Planning

The administrative department that should be the strongest in a large enterprise, accounting, is the weakest department of Oscar Turcios and presents special problems. Ideally the accounting department allows administrators to control the entire firm and other administrative departments. It should provide information to alert the director and other administrators to problems and

20. Interview with William Lezcano, manager of economics, February 1985.
21. Interview with Denis Espinoza, internal auditing, February 1985.

Table 4  *Oscar Turcios: Income Statement,*
*Tobacco, 1984–1985 Agricultural Season*
*(in córdobas)*

| | |
|---|---|
| Earnings | 68,486.9 |
| Less | |
| Agricultural costs | 60,486.9 |
| Preindustrial costs | 17,897.5 |
| Administrative costs | 30,053.7 |
| | (39,951.2) |
| ENIPEX Commission | 684.9 |
| Current interest charges | 13,012.6 |
| | (53,648.7) |
| Interest on accumulated debt | 63,681.9 |
| Net income (loss) | (117,330.6) |

SOURCE: Enterprise Oscar Turcios, Economics, February 1985.

present consolidated balance sheets. The accounting department of Oscar Turcios is six months behind and tangled in documents that provide information not to the enterprise's administrators but instead to MIDINRA Central in Managua. It rarely responds to these documents, giving the impression that they are little more than a formality.

The central contradiction of the firm's accountants is that they complete numerous forms each month and yet know very little about the firm. When asked to identify where the enterprise suffered from a lack of control, an accountant replied, "We don't know where there is not control."[22]

By the accountant's own admission, the accounting department has no control of inventory. It likewise lacks detailed production costs. However, there is little incentive for the accounting department to prepare such information—no one within the

22. Interview with Eduardo Zelaya, internal auditing, February 1985.

enterprise ever asks for information. The accounting department is not even invited to participate in the formulation of the firm's annual plan, the technical economic plan (PTE).

The technical economic plan is drafted by the planning department with help from the economics department; it is used principally for obtaining credit. When possible, and to the extent possible, administrators deliberately inflate projected costs to cover "anything unexpected." Nonetheless, given inflation and the problems confronting the enterprise, projected costs are inevitably still under actual costs. Perhaps in part for this reason, few attempt to follow through with the plan. To the extent that they do, it is in physical goals—principally in acreage planted. Many important administrators in the firm, such as the manager of administration, are, however, unfamiliar with the plan. The important thing is to write one up so that the enterprise can receive credit. After that the plan can be forgotten.[23]

## Losses and More Losses

The economic manager of the enterprise offered a view of the firm's revenue and cost structure (Table 4), which approximates the results of the firm's principal activity—tobacco. The results would not differ appreciably if the firm's other crops were included, as these have little financial significance. Several trends are worth highlighting. First, the firm obviously loses a great deal of money under its present management. Second, administrative costs are exceedingly high—43 percent of revenues and 24 percent of total costs. Third, interest on the firm's accumulated debt almost equals its revenues. Given the absence of a profit margin, next year's interest charges will only be higher. The enterprise is caught in a vicious financial circle.

Actually the income statement is only a projection of revenues and costs. The economic manager believes that revenues may fall short of expectations. The firm has a good crop, but an inordinate amount of tobacco has been damaged from poor handling.[24] In the 1983–1984 agricultural season, total credit received actually

23. Ibid.
24. Interview with William Lezcano, manager of economics, February 1985.

exceeded the value of production. The firm managed to repay only 29 percent of the credit extended for the year.

The financial status of the firm is even more disconcerting, given that the firm does not include a cost (shadow price) for land or an imputed cost for the depreciation for buildings and machinery. Also, in contrast to such commodities as sugar, the international price of tobacco is held to be good, having risen over the last few years. Although the central problem facing the firm has been a rapid escalation of costs, it should be remembered that profits depend as much on revenues as costs. In tobacco more than most agricultural commodities, revenues depend more on quality than sheer volume. The price for damaged dark tobacco is heavily discounted. According to an agricultural technician with considerable experience at the enterprise, both the volume and quality of tobacco produced on the estates have fallen since the state assumed responsibility for production.[25]

Despite the firm's losses, one can expect that next year the firm will continue as if there were no losses. Indeed one could even be led to believe there were profits on the basis of projected investments. The firm continues because of continued support from the nationalized financial system. Any time the enterprise needs additional funding to cover losses, it simply asks its bank for more money. The bank may complain and demand an explanation, but the bank always gives more money. The firm's plea is usually the same, "If we do not receive additional funding, we will lose the harvest." Implicit in this exchange is that the firm is a state enterprise and that obstructing a state enterprise (even with another state enterprise) is tantamount to obstructing the government.

For the most part, the attitude of the firm's administrators toward these losses is the same as that held in the countryside: if the state were to pay a higher price for tobacco there would be no losses. The perception is that the firm loses but that the government gains dollars. It is true that the enterprise has to buy many of its spare parts on the black market; but no one has stopped to figure what percentage of total costs these purchases constitute. By far the greatest cost is labor; many imports are

25. Interview with Freddy Valdiva, technician, February 1985.

available to the firm at prices based on the official exchange rate. Thus, although there is some basis for the enterprise's argument for a higher price, it is a rather facile and misleading approach to solving the firm's financial problems.

At least in the short term, the outlook for Oscar Turcios is not encouraging. The firm faces a multitude of problems, many of which lie outside its control. Oscar Turcios has a new director, however, one who is held in high esteem by administrators, staff, and those in the countryside. He has attempted to change the attitude of the firm—not "to produce at whatever cost" but "to produce with efficiency."[26] It is a difficult task.

26. Interview with Hector Valdivia, director, February 1985.

# 4

## The Enterprise Camilo Ortega

You will not receive your salary until you
turn in your report.
— José "Chepe" Barcenas, director of
Camilo Ortega

Half an hour's drive from Managua is the small city of
Masaya, the center of artisanal activity in Nicaragua. Along with
its embroidery, hammocks, leather goods, and sundry household
products, the Masaya region has long been characterized by the
peasants' small holdings that surround the town and produce
fruits and vegetables for Managua's sprawling markets. On the
eve of the revolution the environs of Masaya, like other regions,
also contained large estates. A number of them, notably those
owned by the Bolaños family, produced cotton for export.

Masaya suffered some of the heaviest fighting and periodic
shootouts between Somoza's National Guard and the Sandinistas. Then, three weeks into what proved to be the "final offensive," Sandinista guerrilla columns were forced to pull out of
Managua and retreat to Masaya. The National Guard laid siege
to the city, a siege that lasted for six weeks, until Somoza fled the
country. Many residents of Masaya were killed in the fighting,
and local resentment of the Somoza regime hardened. Peace
brought hopes for reconstruction and prosperity.

## Founding of the Enterprise Camilo Ortega

The confiscation of the land of Somoza and his associates gave the hastily organized INRA responsibility for many estates around Masaya. There were large tracts, to be sure, and a large number of medium- and small-sized estates that pursued a wide range of activities. While INRA struggled to establish itself, workers and a few managers ran the estates as best they could.

In December 1980 the confiscated estates in the area were organized into a single state farm, named after the brother of Daniel and Humberto Ortega, Camilo, who was killed during the insurrection. Since the two surviving Ortegas were powerful FSLN comandantes, the newly organized enterprise inherited a certain luster. Otherwise, though, the enterprise began with the same disadvantages that every agrarian state enterprise confronted: dispersed and diverse land holdings, accumulated debt, ill-defined objectives, no administrative structure, next to no working capital (C$20,000 [córdobas] for Camilo Ortega), and a shortage of skilled personnel.

The management of Camilo Ortega was assigned to José "Chepe" Barcenas, a guerilla fighter who held the confidence of the Sandinista leadership. Barcenas was a lawyer by training, with no formal background in administration, but his family, unmistakably "bourgeois," was a noted producer of cotton. Barcenas proved to be a superb administrator, instilling pride and responsibility in Camilo Ortega's workers and making the enterprise the most profitable of MIDINRA's hundred-odd state farms.

## Organizing the New Enterprise

At the outset Barcenas defined the objective of Camilo Ortega: "to produce but without losses to the enterprise."[1] He took this step independently with no pressure from MIDINRA Central, any other branch of government, or the workers of

---

1. Interview with Carlos Espinoza, assistant director, February 1985.

Camilo Ortega. The setting of a single objective for the enterprise served as both rationale and guide for the countless daily decisions Barcenas subsequently made in managing Camilo Ortega.

The commitment to avoid losses prompted Barcenas to be careful about the tasks he accepted. Early on, he took a detailed inventory of the firm's resources and activities and then gave away—to landless peasants—small parcels, including all those raising more than one crop.[2] Barcenas defended the unusual measure by arguing that the firm could not efficiently manage small parcels.

Concomitantly, Barcenas decided to concentrate on certain crops and avoid others. His calculations suggested that cotton was the most profitable commodity for the enterprise and that vegetables and basic grains might even be sources of loss. Accordingly, he expanded the cultivation of cotton at the expense of foodcrops. He was especially eager to halt the production of beans because this harvest was often rifled by peasants and poor laborers, and because state-controlled prices were, in Barcenas's opinion, too low.[3]

The decision not to cultivate foodstuffs angered certain officials in MIDINRA Central. Although MIDINRA did not formally engage in central planning, it was anxious to see the production of food, especially maize and beans, increased. Barcenas's argument that production of maize and beans was not profitable was deemed inappropriate. Still Barcenas held his ground, telling Central, "If you want beans, you come grow them."[4] Barcenas prevailed in part because of his impeccable revolutionary credentials but principally because of MIDINRA's disorganization.

The enterprise's endowment of UPEs partly restrained its range of economic activity. Barcenas was able, through his initiative and determination, to concentrate resources on activities that would enable the firm to fulfill the objective, "to produce without losses to the enterprise." Barcenas reasoned that he could do nothing to influence selling prices for the firm's output,

2. Interview with Silvia González, manager of accounting, February 1985.
3. Interview with María Elena de Núñez, manager of economics, February 1985.
4. Ibid.

which would be set by others, often by MIDINRA. Consequently he concentrated his efforts where he could have some control—production costs and yields. He dedicated himself to organizing the firm so that workers kept production costs to a minimum and obtained the highest yields possible, especially for cotton, the barometer of the enterprise.

Barcenas took care in organizing workers and administrators not only to produce but to produce efficiently. At first it was often not clear how to organize things most prudently, especially relations among different branches of the firm. As problems arose, those involved discussed and developed solutions. While Barcenas showed flexibility in the enterprise's organizational constellation, he clung to two principles. Everyone had to have a clear sense of his or her responsibilities.[5] The size of the firm's administration was to stay relatively small; administrative costs could not exceed 9 percent of the firm's total costs of production.[6] He often denied administrators permission to hire additional personnel or increase wages, in order to keep administrative costs under this limit. Aside from Barcenas himself, no one knew how he had arrived at the figure of 9 percent. Conventional wisdom was that "he just pulled it out of his sleeve."[7]

## The Search for Information

While Barcenas controlled overhead by fiat, minimizing costs and maximizing yields proved to be a mammoth undertaking beset by difficulties. Operations were hampered by the disorder inevitably accompanying revolution. Inputs, from seed to tractor tires, were often unavailable. Labor productivity was much lower than before the revolution. Management problems abounded, many stemming from the sheer size of the firm. The SUCA accounting system was cumbersome and slow and made monitoring the far-flung activities of the enterprise difficult.

5. Interview with Silvia González, manager of accounting, February 1985.
6 Interview with María Elena de Núñez, manager of economics, February 1985.
7. Ibid.

Equally problematic was the laxity of UPE administrators and technicians in providing data; they claimed that they were responsible for production and not for administration.

Barcenas insisted that agronomists and managers of UPEs supply requisite data to the accounting department in a timely fashion. He demanded that agronomists and, especially, managers of UPEs know and report their production costs to the firm's economic department, which Barcenas oversaw. Barcenas berated his field staff at meetings, announcing, "A *técnico* who does not know his production costs is of no use to the enterprise; it is better that he leave the enterprise."[8] Several disgruntled administrators did just that, but those who remained began to develop at least crude measures of their departments' costs. To the laggards Barcenas would on occasion write memos that stated, "With this memorandum you are notified that you will not receive your salary until you turn in your report."[9] The memos worked.

Barcenas took the firm's annual technical plan as seriously as he did its accounting. He strove to make the technical plan, which committed the firm to goals in production (but not revenue), as realistic as possible. Headquarters in Masaya did not simply write up the plan; it asked managers of UPEs to contribute their respective goals, which headquarters then aggregated. The staff of UPEs often suggested overly ambitious targets, anticipating the generous provision of additional resources from the firm or from MIDINRA Central. Barcenas would bluntly ask, "How can you propose that? Where will the necessary resources come from? Be realistic. Plan on the basis of what resources you have."[10] Throughout the year Barcenas would attempt to follow the technical plan, reminding his staff of what the firm had committed itself to produce.

Despite the accounting department's plethora of forms for MIDINRA Central, Barcenas nonetheless kept the accounts as up to date as possible.[11] For the most part he relied on quiet encouragement, but he is remembered once to have shouted, "I

8. Ibid.
9. Interview with Silvia González, manager of accounting, February 1985.
10. Interview with María Elena de Núñez, manager of economics, February 1985.
11. Interview with Carlos Espinoza, assistant director, February 1985.

should put a neutron bomb in here [the accounting department], which would kill all of you and just leave the papers and the desks." The accounting department never was—as is said in Nicaragua—*al día* (up to date), but it came to be only two or three months behind. Among MIDINRA's enterprises, that was judged to be a notable accomplishment. Furthermore, Camilo Ortega used annual auditors, a practice followed by only one other MIDINRA enterprise.

Where Barcenas put his greatest attention was on gathering and analyzing production costs in the economics department. In effect, he devised an alternative to the accounting department. Here he obtained data that were less exact and less comprehensive but, because he could delineate and quickly get the information he wanted, ultimately more useful for managerial purposes. Normally, within MIDINRA's enterprises data on production costs and yields were compared—if used at all—with the estimates set forth in the technical plan. That comparison was routinely made in Camilo Ortega; in addition, the data Barcenas collected through the firm's economic department were also used as a basis of comparison among parts of the firm, usually UPEs.[12]

Comparing the economic performance of divisions of the firm offers three important advantages: first, it provides a quicker sense of progress—or its lack. Second, it compares present plans with present costs, which is useful when—as in postrevolutionary Nicaragua—inflation is high but unpredictable, and annual plans lose much of their comparative value. Third, its internal comparisons can hold exogeneous influences constant. If the annual plan assumes average weather and the weather proves to be atypical, for example, comparisons with the annual plan lose merit but remain useful within the firm, since everyone there experiences the same atypical weather.

Internal comparisons of costs and yields in Camilo Ortega are done with a simple matrix. On one axis are listed UPEs that are comparable because they are cultivating the same crop with the same technology. On the other axis are listed data to be examined—costs or yields. Totals are listed but for comparative purposes they are converted to average costs or yields per

12. Ibid.

manzana. Of course, the more UPEs to be compared, the more useful a matrix is. But the matrix depends on similarities in both economic activities of UPEs and technologies they employ.

Table 5 is a matrix used at Camilo Ortega. The enterprise has six UPEs devoted to cultivating cotton, permitting internal monitoring of each UPE by simply comparing it with its brethren. Below the data on the six UPEs is a row computing the averages. The last line of the matrix (actually not part of it) shows projected costs, drawn from the technical plan. Thus the matrix lets the viewer quickly compare the performance of each UPE with that of other similarly situated UPEs and with the UPE's own plan. Of course, the usefulness of the matrix depends on the extent to which it influences managerial decision making.

## Decision Making

Table 5 is a consolidated matrix, one of the simplest ones used at Camilo Ortega. Most matrices are much more detailed, tracing out step by step the cultivation of crops or the management of livestock. Typically a matrix begins on a huge blackboard at the firm's headquarters. Managers of UPEs and agricultural technicians are called to a meeting where they dutifully report their costs and, when appropriate, their yields. Any incongruencies or problems are quickly noted and discussed. For example, a manager of a UPE might be asked why he is using 20 percent more gasoline per manzana than his neighbor. Or he might be asked why labor costs at his UPE are higher for a particular task than at a third UPE.[13]

The practice is not to spend too much time analyzing problems but instead to concentrate on finding solutions. Often those responsible are simply asked, "How are you going to solve your problem?" Thus field administrators are given an opportunity to participate in finding solutions, and responsibility for implementing them remains localized. At the same time the problem is made public, and all are encouraged to offer suggestions. If a UPE has a problem, an effort is made to solve the problem with the resources

13. Ibid.

Table 5  Camilo Ortega: Cost of Cotton Production, 1984 Agricultural Season (in córdobas)

| UPE | Area (in mz) | Machinery | | Labor | | Inputs | | Total Cost Before Harvest[a] | |
|---|---|---|---|---|---|---|---|---|---|
| | | Total | Per mz | Total | Per mz | Total | Per mz | Total | Per mz |
| Matildina | 560 | 559,073 | 998 | 1,034,936 | 1,848 | 2,958,529 | 5,283 | 4,522,533 | 8,129 |
| San Blas | 792 | 555,968 | 761 | 1,818,723 | 2,296 | 3,884,038 | 4,904 | 6,258,730 | 7,902 |
| Rio Verde | 725 | 561,929 | 775 | 1,254,961 | 1,730 | 3,365,579 | 4,642 | 5,182,440 | 7,148 |
| El Porvenir | 870 | 610,839 | 702 | 1,154,601 | 1,327 | 4,753,508 | 5,463 | 6,518,949 | 7,493 |
| Sto. Domingo | 708 | 491,701 | 694 | 1,739,176 | 2,456 | 3,127,957 | 4,418 | 5,358,786 | 7,568 |
| San Cristobal | 360 | 339,750 | 943 | 287,512 | 798 | 1,742,278 | 4,839 | 2,369,542 | 6,582 |
| Total | 4,015 | 3,119,263 | 776 | 7,289,856 | 1,815 | 19,831,890 | 4,939 | 30,241,010 | 7,532 |
| Planned cost | | | 1,144 | | 1,745 | | 4,023 | | 8,837 |
| Outcome | | Actual cost 32% lower than planned cost | | Actual cost 4% higher than planned cost | | Actual cost 23% higher than planned cost | | Actual cost 2% higher than planned cost | |

SOURCE: Enterprise Camilo Ortega, Administration, February 1985.
[a]The cost is as of 12 December 1984 and does not include administrative cost.

of the UPE, not the resources of the firm, MIDINRA's regional office, or MIDINRA Central.

The efficacy of the meetings (as a rule, held every two weeks) and of the matrices that emerge depend on the reliability of information presented. For example, individuals may not wish to report cost overruns or instances of poor productivity. The accounting department verifies information offered to the economics department or to the director himself. Given the backlog in the accounting department, it cannot immediately check figures but can verify them within a reasonable amount of time.[14] Barcenas made it clear to his field staff that figures were to be checked with the accounting department, and that whereas many mistakes could be forgiven, dishonesty could not.

At the UPEs many problems emerge, some that can be resolved and others that are more persistent. The more manageable problems involve use and care of inputs and machinery. The most difficult and enduring problems relate to labor. Shortages interrupt the rhythm of activity; field laborers are said "not to work well—they leave [the fields] sometimes."[15] Laborers resist working for piece wages. They occasionally steal small items from the firm—sacks, barrels, and the like. Workers nominally have a union, which is not effectual, perhaps in part because "the role of the union is not clear."[16]

UPE managers who are unable to maintain production and control costs do not last long at Camilo Ortega. The same holds for agricultural technicians. During his first year as director, Barcenas fired many managers and technicians, including some who were said to be "disastrous." Barcenas promoted eagerly within the firm, ignoring a worker's age, sex, political commitment, and schooling in favor of actual ability. The majority of Camilo Ortega's agricultural technicians came to be *técnicos empíricos,* technicians with no formal training but considerable experience.[17]

14. Interview with Silvia González, manager of accounting, February 1985.
15. Interview with the record keeper for cotton in the UPE Santo Domingo, February 1985.
16. Ibid.
17. Interview with María Elena de Núñez, manager of economics, February 1985.

Salaries for both field workers and administrators are set by the government. They are periodically adjusted for inflation but are nonetheless widely held to lag behind it. In an attempt to buttress real incomes, Camilo Ortega has a long-standing policy of selling food and clothing to workers at subsidized prices.[18] The firm once went so far as to help especially valued employees purchase refrigerators, hoping to stimulate workers to be more diligent and responsible. To that end, the firm presents awards to outstanding workers; workers think awards inadequate as an incentive but still appreciate them.

Barcena's style of managing personnel, collecting and evaluating information, and making decisions has proved useful. It has shown senior administrators what is happening throughout the firm and quickly identified problems and possible solutions. It has informed lower-level administrators—those in the field— what is happening, what their counterparts are doing, and how to participate in solving problems. Most important, though, it continually reinforces responsibilities, goals, and the simple sentiment that "things matter."

## Building Pride, Responsibility, and Profitability

Barcenas worked hard at organizing and managing Camilo Ortega. His normal working hours were from seven in the morning until nine in the evening; often he would be at headquarters until eleven at night. He took the success of the firm with the utmost seriousness, treating it, as one of his associates put it, "as if it were his own." Indeed, on occasion he borrowed machinery from his family's estate for use at Camilo Ortega.[19]

Barcenas was often held to be too demanding, too rough. He was accused of being gross, a brute, and worse. But even those with sharp words for him admired and respected him. He was held

18. Interview with Carlos Espinoza, assistant director, February 1985.
19. Interview with María Elena de Núñez, manager of economics, February 1985.

to "multiply himself a thousand times."[20] His ability to motivate others was said to be mystical. Beyond their regard for his sheer capacity for work and his ability to get things done, their praise for Barcenas centers on three qualities. He took care to teach those who were willing to learn. As rough as he sometimes was with discipline, this was held to be a vital contribution—as one administrator put it, "If there is no control, people will do whatever they please."[21] Finally, he acknowledged and rewarded good work.

Under Barcenas's leadership, Camilo Ortega came to be respected as a well-run enterprise that lent a degree of prestige to the revolution. Employees of Camilo Ortega, at least those with responsibility, took pride in the enterprise. As one administrator said, "We all feel as if Camilo Ortega is ours."[22] Within MIDINRA, Camilo Ortega was acknowledged for its ability to resolve its problems with its own resources. In Masaya itself, Camilo Ortega was likewise respected. Checks from the enterprise were accepted because, unlike many of MIDINRA's other firms, Camilo Ortega did not write checks unless it had funds to cover them.

Successfully managing Camilo Ortega was no small accomplishment. The firm was enormous; its holdings were often in flux, perhaps because it was located in one of the most populous departments of Nicaragua. In 1983 Camilo Ortega received a large and far-flung dairy enterprise, weighted down with debt. Camilo Ortega distributed much of the livestock, with or without land, to cooperatives, only to find the recipients unwilling to pay the accompanying debt. Members refused to view the livestock and land as anything but a "gift." Furthermore, Camilo Ortega found the management of its remaining dairy holdings a continual headache.[23]

Thanks to its location, Camilo Ortega has been only minimally affected by the counterrevolution; some employees, including valued accountants, have been drafted. One agricultural technician refused to come to Masaya out of fear the army would

20. Interview with Carlos Espinoza, assistant director, February 1985.
21. Interview with Sandra Zepeda, manager of planning, February 1985.
22. Ibid.
23. Ibid.

dragoon him into military service.[24] But these problems pale before the difficulties confronting those enterprises along the country's border. Still, most of Nicaragua's state enterprises, including the most unprofitable, are not in war zones.

## The Bottom Line

As of 1985 Camilo Ortega managed fifty-four thousand manzanas, roughly half of them used only for pasturing thirteen thousand head of cattle.[25] Another eight thousand manzanas are in forest, and ten thousand manzanas of potentially farmable land were not in cultivation. Thus, most of Camilo Ortega's land was idle or underused. The land in use was organized into seven complexes, in turn broken down into twenty-four UPEs. All together, the firm comprised fifty-seven confiscated estates, some perhaps without cultivated land. The firm normally had just under one thousand employees, but at the height of the cotton harvest the firm could employ as many as three thousand workers.

As a result of Barcenas's management, the huge enterprise— one of MIDINRA's largest—earned a profit. The firm was in the red at the close of the 1981–1982 agricultural season, but the following year it was in the black, with a net profit of C$243,000. In the 1983–1984 agricultural season it earned a handsome profit of C$5,500,000, making it *the* success among MIDINRA's state farms.[26] Part of the profit the firm used to retire debt, but it held most for use as working capital. Barcenas's idea was for the firm to raise its own working capital and thus be free of the cost (from interest) of annually borrowing working capital. The idea was said to have been approved by Commander Wheelock.

In 1984 "Chepe" Barcenas resigned as director of Camilo Ortega and accepted an administrative position with the Nicaraguan airline, Aeronica. He left Camilo Ortega in good shape, finan-

24. Ibid.
25. Ministry of Agricultural Development and Agrarian Reform (MIDINRA), "Directorio" (Managua, 1984, Mimeographed), p. 41; Enterprise Camilo Ortega, "Plan técnico" (Masaya, 1984, Mimeographed).
26. Interview with María Elena de Núñez, manager of economics, February 1985.

cially and otherwise; but he himself was ill, suffering from a bad ulcer. (It was not clear whether Barcenas's ulcer was caused by the stress of managing Camilo Ortega or by his fondness for rum.) His departure caused many to wonder whether Camilo Ortega could sustain its success. Those within and outside the firm had always traced its success to Barcenas's exceptional leadership.

## An Uncertain Future

Barcenas's replacement, Raúl Barrios, is held to be competent but to lack the former's dynamism. The firm continues to be managed in more or less the same way, in part because the assistant director, Carlos Espinoza, is committed to Barcenas's management style. Still, Barcenas's absence is being felt. For example, administrative costs have not been monitored with the same rigor and have already crept above their 9 percent ceiling; the accounting department has fallen behind in its record keeping. The firm was barely in the black at the conclusion of the 1984–1985 agricultural season. The explanation for the drop in profits was that "costs rose faster than selling prices."[27]

Beginning in the 1985–1986 agricultural season, Camilo Ortega faced another challenge: a mandate from MIDINRA to substitute the cultivation of basic grains for cotton. This request, which the firm did not contest, posed two challenges. The first was simply the physical switch of one crop for another. The second was to produce a profit on maize and beans, crops held to have lower profit margins than cotton.[28] Between the loss of Barcenas and the switch to cultivation of basic grains, it is unclear whether the enterprise Camilo Ortega can maintain its reputation as both the most profitable and the best managed state enterprise in Nicaragua.

27. Ibid.
28. Ibid.

# 5

# The Enterprise Commander Marcos Somarriba

The revolution is beautiful—it's the disorder
that screws everything up.
— Orlando Luques, director of Marcos
Somarriba

The most isolated and neglected region of Nicaragua is undoubtedly the department of Río San Juan, located in the southeastern corner of the country. Western Nicaragua, where the bulk of the country's populace lives, is marked by a cordillera of volcanoes between the Gulf of Fonseca and Lake Nicaragua. These volcanoes protrude from a large structural rift that forms a long narrow depression passing to the southeast.

The rift is occupied in part by the largest freshwater lakes in Central America: Managua (56 kilometers long and 24 kilometers wide) and Nicaragua (161 kilometers long and 75 kilometers wide), linked by the Tipitapa River.[1] The southern one, Lake Nicaragua, drains into the San Juan River, which flows to the Caribbean. For some of its length, the river provides the bound-

---

1. Mary Helms, "The Society and its Environment," in *Nicaragua: A Country Study,* ed. James Rudolph (Washington, D.C.: Department of the Army, U.S. Government, 1981), p. 66.

ary between Nicaragua and Costa Rica. It also gives the department its name.

The San Juan valley forms a natural low-lying passageway across the Nicaraguan isthmus from the Caribbean to Lake Nicaragua. The southwestern edge of Lake Nicaragua is only nineteen kilometers from the Pacific Ocean.[2] During the 1850s the Panamanian route was the most popular way to cross between the Atlantic and Pacific coasts of the United States, but the shorter, cheaper, and healthier Nicaraguan route challenged it for a few years. In Nicaragua's more northerly route, the climate was said to be cooler, and passengers were less exposed to the risk of tropical fevers. None other than Cornelius Vanderbilt ran the transit company shuttling passengers from coast to coast. Mark Twain made the trip in 1866 and described it as a "jolly little scamper across the isthmus."[3]

Engineers had always considered this Nicaraguan route the most practical site for a canal across the isthmus. At several times designs were drawn up, but each time they were frustrated by political squabbling. Because of politics, in the end the canal was built in Panama. International rivalry and local bickering over the site of the canal thus incidentally retarded the development of the San Juan valley.

With the construction of the Panamanian railway and later the canal itself, the San Juan valley fell into oblivion. It was never colonized, and the settlements at either end of the river—San Carlos on Lake Nicaragua and San Juan del Norte on the Caribbean—were small shantytowns. After World War II, cattle ranches were slowly established in areas cleared of tropical forest. The region remained inaccessible to overland vehicles, with transportation limited to boats plying the lakes and the river. The seven ranches that hugged the river reached enormous size but stretched only a third of the way toward the coast. A few laborers managed large herds of cattle, which grazed at will as if they were in the wild. Ranchers also settled some of the larger islands near the southeastern end of Lake Nicaragua.

2. Frederic Rosengarten, Jr., *Freebooters Must Die!* (Wayne, Pa.: Haverford House, 1976), pp. 57–70.
3. Ibid., p. 63.

## Revolution and Expropriation

The somnolence of the San Juan valley ended with the Nicaraguan Revolution. There was no actual fighting in the region (although arms and supplies were ferried across the river from Costa Rica). With the triumph of the FSLN-led insurrection, however, ownership of the entire valley passed to the state. Most of the area was affected by the initial decrees confiscating the assets of Somoza and his associates; *el general,* as Somoza was known in the region, is said to have been the largest landowner. Other land is said to have been abandoned at the onset of the FSLN's final offensive. The owners never returned, leaving the land to be expropriated by the state.

The revolutionary government hastily established an organization to manage and develop all the land in the San Juan valley. This organization, the Enterprise Río San Juan, was based in San Carlos under the jurisdiction of MIDINRA. It was responsible for an enormous tract of land—nobody knew how many manzanas; much of it was in tropical forest, especially near the Caribbean coast. All of the farms had been owned by absentee landlords, facilitating their occupation by the enterprise, which centered attention on the cattle ranches. There was no sabotage, but some livestock was believed to have been spirited across the Costa Rican border.

The Río San Juan enterprise assumed control over a number of small ranches on the islands in Lake Nicaragua that lie close to San Carlos. In addition, the firm received a few unsettled keys and an island planted entirely in avocados, watered by a well-developed irrigation system; no one remembered who had owned the avocados, other than that he was "a famous millionaire."[4]

The firm was hastily organized, but it rather quickly established order on the confiscated estates because their activities were simple and many workers who remained knew more or less what to do. Work slowed, to be sure, and such activities as mending fences stopped. No thought was given to using the

---

4. Interview with workers on the island of La Juana, June 1985.

estates for anything other than cattle grazing, but there was a great deal of uncertainty as to how to manage the estates.

In fact, the enterprise never defined exactly how to organize and manage its operations. The firm had no specific objectives and no strategy; it made decisions on a day-to-day basis, with little effort at continuity. The state financial system provided funding to stimulate production, and the money was spent as problems arose. No one bothered to keep records of any kind. Personnel came and went, with many administrators staying for only two or three months. The firm's first director abruptly fled to Costa Rica.

For three years, the company operated with no accounting system to assess whether the enterprise was efficiently using the resources with which it had been entrusted. Finally, in the middle of 1982, a team of auditors and accountants arrived from MIDINRA Central in Managua. They set up an accounting system and pieced together a balance statement. It showed assets of C$158 million, balanced by C$60 million in equity and C$99 million in debts to the national banking system. A small part of the C$99-million debt (equivalent to 63 percent of all assets) had been inherited from the confiscated farms, and another part represented investments, but the majority of the debt was deemed to be an unrecoverable loss from the initial three years of state management.[5] How and why the firm came to have such a large debt proved impossible to delineate.

## Creation of the Enterprise Commander Marcos Somarriba

In December 1983 MIDINRA Central, believing that the enterprise was simply too large, divided it in two. The undeveloped eastern half was reorganized into a separate firm and named Hilario Sánchez. The cattle estates around San Carlos were to be retained under the Río San Juan enterprise, but the now leaner enterprise was renamed Commander Marcos Somarriba. Where-

5. Interview with Orlando Luques, director, June 1985.

as the assets of the Río San Juan enterprise were divided between the two entities, the Marcos Somarriba firm was saddled with all of its debt. The rationale for this decision was that Marcos Somarriba had the bulk of the productive assets; the debt had been run up in reactivating and managing those assets. The administrators of Marcos Somarriba have always maintained that the assignment of the entire debt to their enterprise was unjust.

Even after the split, the reorganized firm at San Carlos is huge. It possesses 85,868 manzanas, making it one of the largest agricultural enterprises (in area) in Nicaragua.[6] Slightly over 60 percent of the land consists of uncleared brush or forest. Roughly 27 percent of the land is in pasture, the bulk of it cultivated pasture. The majority of the remaining land is cleared of brush but fallow. Only a fraction of 1 percent of total land—140 manzanas—is planted in perennial and annual crops; the former include cacao and avocados and the latter are mostly vegetables.

Since its inception, the enterprise has maintained about 16,500 head of cattle, with more than a manzana of pasture available per animal. If the presently unused land is added to this pasturage, there are roughly five manzanas per head of cattle. In the San Juan River valley it is held that a manzana of cultivated pasture can adequately accommodate three head of cattle throughout the year, suggesting underutilization of the land.

The firm is organized into three complejos, which in turn consist of UPEs that are productively similar or in proximity to one another. For example, one complejo is composed of two large cattle ranches near enough to San Carlos to allow the use of agricultural machinery. A second complejo consists of the other five cattle ranches spread out along the San Juan River from the banks of the river to the Costa Rican border. (Further south the river itself forms the border.) The third complejo groups the island farms in the lake. Two of its UPEs are cattle ranches; the other five grow permanent and annual crops. Each complejo has its administrative center in one of its UPEs—in particular, the one that has the best living conditions. In two instances this is also the UPE with the greatest economic importance.

6. Ministry of Agricultural Development and Agrarian Reform (MIDINRA), "Directorio" (Managua, 1984, mimeographed).

When the estates were confiscated, they had few improvements. To be sure, there were barbed-wire fences, horses, and a few corrals. The largest estate had some equipment, an above-ground fuel tank, boats of varying sizes, assorted buildings, an elegant home overlooking the river, and a pet jaguar (chained to a stake). Another estate had a large comfortable home that the former owner used during his visits. The remaining estates had only slovenly quarters for the few workers who attended the cattle. Since the revolution the beautiful home with the pet jaguar has been designated a protocol residence for visiting government dignitaries (the jaguar is still chained to its stake); the other large home is used as an FSLN school for the political training of cadres.

What the enterprise found it had inherited was an eclectic array of boats; the most valuable was a large vessel, apparently built to haul vehicles. A wide gate at the bow lowers to serve as a bridge into the open hull. The boat also pulls a barge that functions as a floating metal corral. Together the two craft can transport seventy head of cattle to a makeshift ramp in Granada, at the other end of Lake Nicaragua, only an hour's drive to Managua. The trip takes from twenty-five to thirty hours, depending on the weather.

The enterprise also inherited half a dozen smaller boats, each seemingly having a different brand of outboard motor. These provide transportation among the enterprise's UPEs, and between the San Juan valley and the more populous Pacific zone of Nicaragua. There is also a beat-up Suzuki jeep, but it is only good for visiting two UPEs; even for that it is slower than a boat.

Comparable to the poverty of the enterprise's equipment and facilities (not only in absolute terms but compared to the Pacific zone) is the paucity of labor in general, and of educated labor in particular. Although the Sandinista literacy campaign reached some of the manual laborers, nearly all seem to have returned to functional illiteracy, unable to do more than sign their name. Rural laborers in the area are also noted for their penchant for periodic relocation. Few have the attitude of one of the firm's workers that "there is no point in moving around because you eat rice and beans in every hacienda."

An especially serious problem is the flight of workers to Costa

Rica. Laborers reportedly leave for economic rather than political reasons, claiming that they can buy a pair of pants with what they earn from two days of work in Costa Rica, whereas for the same pair of pants they would have to work a month in Nicaragua. A few have also fled to Costa Rica to avoid Nicaragua's obligatory military service. Laborers from outside the San Juan valley have reportedly come to work for the enterprise, only to use it as a "trampoline" to cross into Costa Rica.[7]

By all accounts, laborers in the valley have little interest in politics. As local FSLN cadres say, workers have an "underdeveloped political consciousness"; they are hardy and brave but occupied primarily by selfish concerns. Despite the reorganization of the ranches into a state enterprise, the workers seem to feel that their situation has changed little since the revolution. They routinely refer to the firms as haciendas and to the director of each UPE as the patrón. More important, workers are not interested in the profitability of the enterprise since they earn the same no matter what the firm earns—or loses.[8] Their lack of education and political consciousness is yet another result of the historical isolation and neglect of the San Juan valley.

Management of the Enterprise Marcos Somarriba is made all the more difficult by counterrevolutionary forces whose guerrilla columns have penetrated as far as the outskirts of San Carlos. In 1983 an attack launched on the firm's most important UPE resulted in heavy losses. In early 1985 Luques, the firm's director, and four of his staff were caught in an ambush; there were no fatalities but the manager of a UPE was wounded. A recurring problem has been the theft of cattle, especially from UPEs bordering Costa Rica. By 1985 the total loss of cattle was estimated at fifteen hundred animals.[9]

The burden of the counterrevolution has not only wrought direct losses but has also created a climate of fear and uncertainty in the firm that exacts a cost even when all appears normal. Many employees, especially administrators, have learned how to handle weapons, and UPEs always have AK-47s at the ready. Not surprisingly, the job of recruiting personnel for the

---

7. Interview with Fernando Romero, manager of production, June 1985.
8. Interview with workers at the UPE El Salvador, June 1985.
9. Interview with Orlando Luques, director, June 1985.

enterprise from outside the valley is nearly impossible. A typical response is "No, brother, I'm not bored with life yet."

To meet the threat of the counterrevolution, the Sandinista army has stationed small contingents of troops at several of the firm's UPEs, in particular those bordering Costa Rica. (The practice is common along both the northern and southern borders of the country.) The troops serve both to impede the movement of guerrilla columns and to defend the firm's employees and facilities. The troops have improvised their own shelter, which is rarely more than a simple roof, since they sleep in hammocks. They are fed by the enterprise, though, and eat with the workers.

The firm would never impede the deployment of the Sandinista army, since defense is unquestionably paramount. A common slogan in postrevolutionary Nicaragua is "everything for defense." Still, the stationing of troops at the firm's UPEs is a mixed blessing. The evidence is unclear as to whether the presence of troops thwarts or invites attacks by guerrillas on state farms. But laborers at Marcos Somarriba's UPEs will not venture into unsettled areas with the troops and will not carry arms. Less consequential but nonetheless relevant are the petty problems caused by the troops: the extra expense and chore of supplying provisions, the occasional quarrel between a soldier and a laborer, and such nuisances as the shooting of a prized bull by a bored soldier.

Perhaps because of the difficult environment the Marcos Somarriba firm confronts, it has experienced high turnover among administrative personnel. In its first five years it has had four directors, including one who was supposedly so taken aback by the problems in the UPEs that he would not leave his office in San Carlos. Likewise, the firm has had five head accountants; similar turnover has occurred at the UPEs. The high rotation of administrators makes it difficult to address the urgent problems facing the enterprise or even to devise ways of living with them.

## Managing amidst Hardship

In 1985 the firm found some stability with the appointment of a veterinarian, Orlando Luques, as director. Although Luques has no prior experience in administration, his family owned and managed a cattle ranch in the department of Boaco. Perhaps of equal importance to the minister of MIDINRA, who appoints directors, he is a member of the FSLN. On his appointment, Luques sought the help of several of his friends who had been cattle ranchers in Boaco until they were displaced by the fighting between the Sandinista army and the counterrevolutionaries. His most trusted friend assumed the position of manager of production, while others became directors of the most productive UPEs.

The arrival of Luques's friends evoked considerable criticism from employees. He has been charged with *amigoísmo* and *boacoísmo*. Still, it is readily apparent that the Boacoans are experienced cattle ranchers and hard workers. Ironically, except for Luques the Boacoans lack strong political commitment to the revolution. They are cattle ranchers who simply feel displaced anywhere else than on a cattle ranch. One confided his hope that by working on a government farm he would improve his chances of getting his ranch back once the government had cleared the counterrevolutionaries out of Boaco and the neighboring departments of Chontales and Zelaya.

Even with a staff of thirty-seven at the firm's headquarters in San Carlos and a staff at each UPE, Orlando Luques spends most days out in the countryside. He attempts to stay on top of each UPE's progress and problems. Often he and his "right hand," the production manager, will leave San Carlos in the morning by boat, taking their saddles and Luques's AK-47, to spend the day on a special task at a UPE. A common task is the transfer of cattle from one area to another. Orlando thus spends much of his time doing the work of an ordinary field hand, staying in touch with whatever is going on in the countryside.

Luques avoids spending time in his office because "it is boring" and because he prefers to devote his time to what he sees as the firm's central objective—to raise livestock. Administrative tasks he judges to be bothersome and cumbersome. Worse, there are constant interruptions. For example, one day a stranger walked into his office with a sizable check from the enterprise; the check had bounced. It had been written a year and a half earlier, before Orlando had assumed management of the firm. When the bank finally finished processing the check, there was not enough money in the firm's account to cover it. Luques had to spend the better part of a day negotiating with the bank to make the check good.

## Planning Problems

Nominally the activities of each enterprise are guided by an annual plan, the technical economic plan (PTE). A number of individuals in the firm's department of economics devote considerable time to drawing up the plan, with the administrators of the UPEs also contributing to the process. Yet the plan is used only to secure financing from the San Carlos branch of the National Development Bank. Once the year's financing has been received, the PTE is all but forgotten. Projected costs are based on actual costs at the time of the plan, but inflation quickly wreaks havoc with the financial side of the PTE, making it useless as a budget. Its production goals that should guide the management of the enterprise are virtually ignored. The administrators simply do the best they can, attending to necessities and problems as they arise and as resources permit.[10]

Nonetheless, the firm collects a formidable amount of information, most of it for purposes of control. Information collected on a daily or a weekly basis finds its way to the director in four monthly reports. The statistics department produces a compilation of production data; the accounting department details production costs and cash flow; the warehouse presents an inventory; and the production department gives an overview of the firm's activities. As can be expected, there is considerable overlap among these reports, especially between those by the statistics and production departments. Data provided by the production department are the "freshest" and most complete. The accounting department runs ten to twelve months behind schedule, so that the information it provides is virtually useless for managerial decision making.

The monthly information provided by the production department enables the director to evaluate progress on ongoing activi-

10. Interview with Juan Francisco Hudgson, accounting manager, June 1985.

ties and special projects he has requested UPEs to undertake. Information about the development and movement of livestock commands special attention, since cattle are the source of the firm's earnings as well as its most valuable asset.

While Luques thus receives statistical data to complement the firsthand information gleaned on his visits to the countryside, he lacks information on the rate of financial return of productive activity. Information about costs is sparse and what little exists is not linked to data about earnings. Consequently there is no guide for what to do or avoid and, probably more serious, no factual basis for setting priorities among the resources available. This shortage of information about the economic return on activities exists at all levels of the firm—UPEs, complejos, and the firm as a whole.

## Keeping Accounts

The establishment of an accounting department, however belated, enabled the firm to get an idea of the financial results of its operations and held forth the promise of providing information for managerial decision making. The first income statement prepared was for the 1982–1983 agricultural season, the firm's third year of operations. The recorded balance was a loss of C$7,110,319; but roughly C$4 million worth of supposed accounts receivable never materialized, so that the actual net loss was C$11 million, equivalent to 1 percent of the firm's assets (other than land, which is not valued).[11] Income and expenses were managed in a single account, a "single bag" in the vernacular, which made it impossible to identify why or where the firm lost money.

At the end of the 1983–1984 agricultural season, the enterprise benefited from the arrival of a skilled and dedicated accountant, Francisco Hudgson. He struggled to bring the accounting up to date and improve its reliability. Equally important, he began to break down costs by UPE and by activity. When he had assembled total costs per UPE for the 1983–1984 agricultural

11. Ibid.

season, the accounting department constructed a huge matrix on a roll of newsprint. Measuring four feet by ten feet, the matrix was the central attraction at a large meeting for the firm's employees in San Carlos and for special guests. There was a sense of accomplishment; for the first time, the firm knew where its money was going. The residents of San Carlos who attended the presentation were said to be impressed too; someone claimed, "We thought you had been spending the money like it was from a piñata and stealing it like whores."[12]

Hudgson prepared the year's income statement in a way unorthodox for MIDINRA that showed how each of the firm's activities contributed to the year's results. The bottom line was a loss of nearly C$7 million on sales of C$11 million—a shocking ratio. A breakdown of these results shows that the firm earned money (before allocation of administrative costs) on livestock, while it lost money on cacao, avocados, and vegetables (Table 6).

A more sophisticated presentation would have divided administrative costs among the firm's different activities. It is, in fact, these costs that stand out (Table 7). Administrative costs are C$7 million compared to C$10 million in production costs; administration accounts for a staggering 37 percent of total costs. Nearly 50 percent of the administrative costs were lumped together under "other expenses"; in explaining the figures, the accounting department suggested that interest costs of nearly C$2 million may have been included. Although the department considered that some expenses, such as interest charges, may be mistakenly charged to administration, there is a consensus that administrative costs are in any case too high.

A continued weakness of the firm's accounting is that costs are equated only with cash outlays. Thus, when cattle are stolen or lost, the corresponding cost is not entered in the firm's accounts. Given the magnitude of cattle thefts from the firm, this omission is consequential. Luques is convinced that the drubbing the Sandinista army gave local counterrevolutionaries in 1985 will end the problem—at least for a while, but even an occasional "stray loss" should be recorded in calculating the firm's annual income statement.

12. Interview with Orlando Luques, director, June 1985.

Table 6  Marcos Somarriba: Income Statement, 1983–1984 (in córdobas)

| | Total | Cacao | Vegetables | Avocados | Livestock | Animal Products | Supplies |
|---|---|---|---|---|---|---|---|
| Sale of products | 10,927,373.54 | 269,610.00 | 10,175.00 | 175,807.95 | 10,233,274.09 | 138,506.50 | |
| Sale of supplies | 88.25 | | | | | | 88.25 |
| Total sales | 10,927,461.79 | 269,610.00 | 10,175.00 | 175,807.95 | 10,233,274.09 | 138,506.50 | 88.25 |
| Production costs | 10,132,058.88 | 302,278.80 | 153,364.20 | 1,260,003.49 | 8,417,412.39 | | |
| Cost of supplies | 16,946.00 | | | | | | 16,946.00 |
| Total production costs | 10,149,004.88 | 302,278.80 | 153,364.20 | 1,260,003.49 | 8,417,412.39 | | 16,946.00 |
| Gross earnings | 778,456.91 | (31,668.80) | (143,189.20) | (1,084,195.54) | 1,815,861.70 | 138,506.50 | (16,857.75) |
| Administrative costs | 7,245,464.75 | | | | | | |
| Net earnings (loss) | (6,467,007.84) | | | | | | |
| Other income | 989,663.89 | | | | | | |
| Other expenses | 1,408,183.67 | | | | | | |
| Profit (loss) | (6,885,527.62) | | | | | | |

SOURCE: Enterprise Commander Marcos Somarriba, "Estados financieros ciclo 1983–1984" (San Carlos, 1984, Mimeographed).

Table 7     Marcos Somarriba:
Administrative Costs, 1983–1984
(in córdobas)

| | |
|---|---|
| Materials | 767,239.52 |
| Fuel | 140,302.62 |
| Outside services | 808,883.82 |
| Personnel expenses | 181,725.89 |
| Wages | 1,348,598.63 |
| Social benefits | 522,540.19 |
| Other expenses | 3,476,051.08 |
| Total | 7,245,341.75 |

SOURCE: Enterprise Commander Marcos Somarriba, "Estados financieros ciclo 1983–1984" (San Carlos, 1984, Mimeographed).

A similar confusion over costs exists with depreciation. The
firm does not depreciate assets acquired through confiscation of
the estates that today make up the firm. The firm's investments
in machinery are depreciated, but in a mechanical fashion. For
example, the largest and most productive UPE acquired seven
new Soviet Belrusa tractors at the start of the 1984–1985 agricultural season. Six months later, three tractors were more or less
permanently out of service, with one cannibalized for spare
parts. According to the UPE's mechanic, the problem is that the
Soviet tractors are "shitty"; the director of the firm claims, "The
firm's mechanics know only how to destroy equipment, not fix
it."[13] In any case, no special consideration is made in the firm's
accounts for the loss of the machinery. Even the cannibalized
tractor will be depreciated for another four years.

Despite such problems, the firm's accounting has improved
considerably, but not to the point where accounting data can be
used for managerial decision making. For example, the total
amount of money spent in each UPE does not in itself say much;
without information on each UPE's earnings, the firm cannot tell
if the money was well spent. A UPE with higher than average expenses may have produced a disproportionate share of earnings.

13. Interview with employees of the UPE El Salvador, June 1985.

Comparison of production costs with revenue generated is especially difficult for the firm's principal activity—raising livestock. Cattle are kept by the firm for varying lengths of time, but almost always longer than a single agricultural cycle. How does an administrator measure the value gained by having an animal grazing for a year? Beyond this inherent difficulty, the transfers of animals from one UPE to another for varying reasons cause a complication. No record is kept of these transfers, making it impossible even to estimate the revenue generated by individual UPEs. Not only do managers of UPEs have no idea whether their particular UPEs are profitable, they have no idea whether the firm itself makes or loses money. No one tells them.

Luques did not worry long over the income statement for the 1983–1984 agricultural season: by the time the statement was prepared, inflation had wrought havoc with prices. Costs had risen, but the central government's liberalization of certain commodity prices was expected to aid the firm. The state raised livestock prices in particular—by close to 100 percent. The rise was precipitated by the private sector's failure to deliver livestock to the nation's slaughterhouses, all owned and operated by the government. An alarming share of the livestock was slaughtered clandestinely and sold on the flourishing black market.[14] To combat this trend the government raised prices, even going to the extreme of paying a small fraction of the total price in dollars (paid in cash).

## Shouldering Outside Burdens

The prices for cacao and avocados have also risen dramatically. For example, avocados increased their profit to the firm tenfold in two years. Vegetables, by contrast, have been a source of concern to management. The firm does not cultivate vegetables. Instead it is linked to a nationwide program for food self-sufficiency, known by its acronym PAN. The Marcos Somarriba firm assumes financial responsibility for the program's local activities but has next to no control over its management.

14. *El Nuevo Diario*, 31 July 1985.

San Carlos and its environs depend on the shipment of food (and nearly everything else) across Lake Nicaragua from the populous Pacific departments. The leadership of the PAN program, which is managed with considerable autonomy by MIDINRA, decided that San Carlos should begin to grow foodstuffs. To this end two small islands in Lake Nicaragua named after a tropical fruit, the zapote, were designated for the production of vegetables. A project director was appointed, and the Marcos Somarriba firm was ordered to provide technical and financial assistance. The National Development Bank provided funding, but the loans were made to the firm and not to the project.

After two years of work, the project had made considerable investments in building facilities for workers. The project has difficulty hiring and keeping workers, though. On two occasions, field workers have disappeared in the middle of the night, each time taking one of the project's boats (equipped with an outboard motor). As a consequence of labor shortages, plans for cultivating forty manzanas have gone unfulfilled; only eight manzanas have been planted.[15] Although the foreman (a fugitive Costa Rican) is knowledgeable and experienced, production has been low and of poor quality.

The project director claims that within a few years production will be improved to the point where it will cover costs. Orlando Luques, however, is doubtful. For him the project is a headache and a financial disaster. Perhaps a few crops that require little labor input, such as casava and plantain, might ultimately prove profitable; but the results to date suggest that the firm would be better off abandoning the project. Aggravating his concerns is the realization that many costs incurred have not yet been recorded. For example, a government delegation cleared brush off the islands with a Caterpillar in 1982 but did not get around to billing the firm until 1985—and used 1985 prices.[16]

The dilemma posed by the PAN project is typical of those confronting the director. Supposedly, as director of a firm he is responsible to MIDINRA and to the National Development

15. Interview with the foreman of the PAN project on the islands of El Zapote and El Zapotillo, June 1985.
16. Interview with Orlando Luques, director, June 1985.

Bank for the enterprise's financial success or failure. Yet he lacks the independence commensurate with such responsibility. The firm is burdened by obligations that have little or nothing to do with its central purpose—to produce livestock efficiently.

A similar problem exists with the firm's employees in San Carlos. Despite their relative advantage over workers in the countryside, they are always pressing Luques for special benefits. In particular, they have long urged the firm to open a special commissary providing necessary commodities at "rational prices," a euphemism for subsidized prices. Employees also commonly ask for loans. Even other residents of San Carlos ask for assorted favors that entail costs of one sort or another to the firm. Luques's efforts to deny these requests have more than once elicited the retort that he is a capitalist.[17]

## Conclusion

Orlando Luques, the director of Commander Marcos Somarriba, is deeply committed to the revolution and the responsibility it gives him. He aspires to make the enterprise a vanguard firm, which he defines principally in terms of the political consciousness of its workers but also in terms of productivity and efficiency. He views the counterrevolution as his main obstacle. Despite his constant preoccupation with the counterrevolution, which presents indirect as well as direct costs to the firm, he strives continually to improve the firm's management.

He bases his efforts for the firm on his concern at the firm's gloomy balance sheet. Perhaps surprisingly, Luques's concern is personal; no one in MIDINRA seems to evaluate the firm's progress, let alone complain. The bank officials with whom he negotiates the firm's credit line are sometimes critical, but they always provide credit. Nonetheless, Luques believes that to continue losing money is harmful for a state enterprise. He is determined that people are not going to joke, as they commonly do, that the

17. Ibid.

state sector's acronym, APP, stands for *autorizado para perder* (authorized to be unprofitable).[18]

Efforts to improve the firm's management have ranged from placing a snake in the warehouse (to eat mice and deter thieves) to improving the accounting system. Perhaps most important, though, is establishing the firm as a productive entity. As Luques puts it, "People have to realize that the firm is not an army base, an employment agency, a store, or a bank—it is a cattle enterprise."[19]

18. Ibid.
19. Ibid.

# PART THREE

# 6

# Political Import

The history of the Enterprises Oscar Turcios, Camilo Ortega, and Commander Marcos Somarriba suggests the myriad obstacles confronting those seeking to manage Nicaragua's commanding heights. It evokes sympathy for the director of another enterprise who lamented that his firm "was born bankrupt."[1] The history of the three enterprises also provides an illuminating backdrop for a stark seven-page MIDINRA report that listed twenty-nine "principal causes" for the staggering losses by the ministry's firms.[2] Notwithstanding the length of the list, the problems stated were broadly general. Each one could have been broken down into subsets of difficulties.

Given the environment in which the agrarian APP labors, the behavior reported in the Enterprises Oscar Turcios and Commander Marcos Somarriba is not surprising, even though it often leads to financial loss. In the firm with a profit, the Enterprise Camilo Ortega, it seems unexpected, against the norm (particularly the behavior of the founding director). Understanding this "managerial environment," disaggregating its dimensions, is the best way to explain how and why decisions have been made that—in the end—unknowingly led toward Nicaragua's economic morass. Consideration of the state administrators' environment be-

---

1. Interview with Manuel Duarte, director of the Enterprise Adolfo García Barberena, El Crucero, January 1985.
2. Ministry of Agricultural Development and Agrarian Reform (MIDINRA), "Problemática de las empresas" (Managua, 1985, Mimeographed).

gins with the most obvious and immediate element—the poverty of resources. This poverty is a legacy of the former regime and the insurrection, sorely aggravated in the postrevolutionary epoch by the counterrevolution. But a comprehensive portrait of the state administrators' environment must include a sketch of the influence of politics.

Postrevolutionary Nicaragua has been intensely politicized, circumscribing Sandinista efforts to build a new Nicaragua. While the regime has not hesitated to act, as in establishing the APP, it has continuously weighed its political fortunes in forming and implementing policy. According to Commander Wheelock,

> Since the beginning of this revolution we have not had the elements or objective conditions for the construction of socialism, not in agriculture, not in industry, not in commerce. This is to say, before everything we have to consult history, the socioeconomic evolution of the country, political circumstances, and since 1979 geopolitics, before choosing those factors that will guide us toward an adequate social transformation, one in keeping with the interests of the revolution.[3]

These remarks suggest the influence of politics on decision making. But they do not touch on the extent of the regime's attempts to shape political circumstances. The FSLN actively seeks to retain its supporters, win the uncommitted, and disarm its adversaries. And it calls on state enterprises to participate in this political work. Examples abound, from the provision of employment and social services to the stationing and maintenance of troops. The requirement to perform these tasks, which vary from enterprise to enterprise, affects the managerial environment. At the least it clouds objectives and saps resources.

Politics influences the performance of Nicaragua's state enterprises beyond manipulating them as political resources to fulfill political tasks. That dimension exists and needs to be appreciated. But politics has had another, qualitatively different, impact. The revolution brought a change of attitudes, values, and norms— what might be called a new mentalité. Perhaps the heated rhetoric of the revolution, debasing traditional authority, challenged atti-

3. Jaime Wheelock, *Entre la crisis y la agresión* (Managua: MIDINRA, 1984), p. 7.

tudes toward much that the old order held dear, including accounting, profits, banks, and even a full day's work. The change in attitudes was not complete, evenly shared, necessarily consistent, or enduring. Yet the course of the revolution unmistakably altered attitudes and values, with considerable impact on the performance of state enterprises.

The constellation of these three dimensions in the managerial environment explains in large measure the decisions and resulting outcomes in Nicaragua's Property of the People. Of course there are individual variations and peculiarities. Nonetheless, the impact of poverty, the pursuit of political as well as financial objectives, and the politically inspired reversal of many values, suggest how rational decisions by countless individuals have in the aggregate led to unexpected and undesired results for the Nicaraguan Revolution. The history of the Enterprises Oscar Turcios, Camilo Ortega, and Commander Marcos Somarriba shows that these three dimensions of the administrative environment interact and, more often than not, reinforce one another. As a result, measuring their relative importance is exceedingly difficult, if not impossible. The case of the Enterprise Camilo Ortega hints, though, that whereas poverty may be the most immediate constraint, politics is likely to present more enduring obstacles. Acknowledging their interplay in the managerial environment, the discussion here separates the different components in order to derive propositions.

## Poverty and Aggression

Many of the day-to-day difficulties confronting administrators of the agrarian APP simply result from Nicaragua's poverty. Resources of every type, including administrative skills, are scarce. In addition to the inevitable chaos accompanying the change from private to state ownership, the new-found "enterprises of MIDINRA began to operate without adequate initial capitalization or state support."[4] Once constituted, the enter-

4. MIDINRA, "Problemática de las empresas del sector agropecuario adscritas al MIDINRA" (Managua, 1985, Mimeographed), p. 2.

prises have had considerable and continual needs. The enterprises employ an intermediate level of agroindustrial technology that must have timely delivery of such inputs as fertilizers and insecticides, machinery, gasoline, and spare parts. The size and geographic dispersion of the enterprises necessitate transportation and, above all, accounting, control, and administrative systems—and trained personnel to administer them.

Fulfilling these needs has been problematic. The original intention was that MIDINRA's service enterprises alone meet the material needs of MIDINRA's production-oriented enterprises. That mandate proved impossible to attain and "flexibility was given to enable the agrarian enterprises to contract services from the private sector."[5] But private service firms have suffered some of the same problems as their public counterparts; they lack merchandise because of the shortage of foreign exchange. There are problems with the state-controlled storage and distribution of imported goods.[6] And switching farming input and machinery from capitalist countries to socialist countries has caused problems: finding spare parts for old machinery (John Deere tractors, for example) and using and maintaining new, and hence unfamiliar, products. The counterrevolution has exacerbated difficulties with the balance of payments and imported goods—most noticeably by channeling gasoline and diesel fuel to the army.

The consequences for state enterprises are multifaceted but predictable: production is delayed or less than optimal because inputs are unavailable. Sometimes expensive machinery is idle, lacking spare parts or tires. More commonly, considerable resources, including time, go to finding—and paying for—goods that should be readily available. Often goods can be found only in Managua's "black market," centered in the Mercado Oriental. The Julio Buitrago sugar refinery, for example, buys half of its spare parts in the black market because state agencies cannot provide them. Prices in the black market are high: "You have to pay what they ask."[7] Receipts are hastily written slips of paper.

5. MIDINRA, "La política para el APP" (Managua, 1982, Mimeographed), p. 15, also 14, 16, and 17.

6. *Barricada,* 18 May 1985.

7. Interview with Alberto Gallo, administrator, the Enterprise Julio Buitrago, Masachapa, January 1985.

Adding to their high prices is the cost of searching for materials, in the black market or elsewhere. The Enterprise Oscar Turcios is not alone in opening an office in Managua to find needed inputs and spare parts. Difficulties in obtaining materials, with the common resort to the black market, may also contribute to petty theft and corruption, as suggested by the oblique Nicaraguan proverb, often quoted in discussions of corruption, "Fishermen profit from turbulent waters."

Postrevolutionary Nicaragua's poverty is not limited to material resources. There is a dearth of skilled administrators. The always small pool of experienced managers has shrunk because many have emigrated; perhaps they were identified with Somoza's regime, or they decided that the Nicaraguan Revolution was not in their interests. Yet managerial needs have mushroomed. In addition to a general increase in the number and size of state bureaucracies, the formation of the APP created a score of enterprises of a size matched in Central America only by the legendary banana plantations of U.S. companies.

MIDINRA Central's attempts to implement a uniform administrative system have encountered a host of problems. The enterprises are not only huge but complicated and different from one another. Under these conditions, a standard organization may be impossible. The attempt to impose a uniform administrative system has led to ambiguities about responsibilities; as one enterprise director bluntly said, "Responsibilities are poorly defined."[8] Worse perhaps, MIDINRA Central's efforts have given the enterprises a sense that fault lies with MIDINRA Central. For their part, officials in Managua hold that uniformity is necessary not only for planning but—given the enterprises' limited administrative capability—for organizing the enterprises. Even using Managua's directives, MIDINRA Central senses, "the enterprises have done a thousand different things."[9]

Throughout Nicaragua's state enterprises, accounting makes special difficulties. Since accounting data are used not only for

8. Interview with Eduardo Fonseca, director of the Enterprise ENIA-PROAGRO, Managua, February 1985.

9. Meeting with Silvio Lanuza, director of enterprise management, MIDINRA Central, Managua, February 1985.

control but ideally for guiding decisions, the problems are menacing. Problems can be traced to the sheer volume of activity in most enterprises; the complexity of MIDINRA's accounting system; the inexperience of laborers and technicians in reporting data; the number of reports requested by MIDINRA (and other ministries); and inflation. In the majority of enterprises, accounting is backed up—sometimes a year behind schedule. And despite the specificity that MIDINRA's accounting system demands, in practice firms often keep records only on an aggregate basis, what accountants call "globalized" or "in a single bag." Consequently, firms cannot break down costs or revenues by UPE or activity. Worse, the data that do exist are often unreliable. The result is a void—the absence of data for analysis. As one administrator put it, if you ask an accountant for information about costs he will likely answer, "I am not a magician."[10]

Aside from the enormity of the administrative tasks in establishing the APP, MIDINRA had difficulties in finding qualified personnel to assume the responsibilities. It acknowledged this limitation in an internal ministry document:

> It is not insignificant to note that the experience of the cadres that the ministry has appointed to manage these enterprises is not very great, above all in managing enterprises of the size MIDINRA has; nonetheless, there do not exist in the country cadres who could have done better.[11]

As in the Enterprises Oscar Turcios and Commander Marcos Somarriba, many enterprise directors are agricultural technicians, agronomists, and the like. Lesser ranking administrators in the enterprises also tend to have limited managerial experience—or none. For reasons that are not clear, those with some managerial training and experience tend to move from position to position. Indeed, directors often cite "excessive rotation of personnel" as one of their problems. (And often those who resign fail to give notice.) In the complejos and UPEs, administration is hampered

10. Interview with Manuel Castro and Fidel Olivas, administrators, office of MIDINRA's fourth region, Estelí, January 1985.
11. MIDINRA, "Sistema de dirección de empresas" (Managua, 1984, Mimeographed), p. 4.

by the functional illiteracy of many laborers, including those expected to collect and monitor assorted data.

Nicaragua's material and administrative poverty raises two questions about the APP. The scarcity of inputs, especially those imported, affects private entrepreneurs as well as state enterprises, but it affects state enterprises disproportionately because they employ—on the average—more advanced technology. They must take care to match technology with its cost—and their capacity to pay for it. MIDINRA appears to have strayed from this constraint. Aspirations and initial attempts to employ further advanced technology and to "step up" in the international division of labor appear premature.

The second question concerns economies of scale. Aside from the shortage of imported inputs and the feasibility of heightened technology, the dearth of administrative talent alone diminishes potential economies of scale in the APP. Most state enterprises suffer from a paradox: they have a bloated and costly administration yet cannot manage activities efficiently or even keep track of them. A ranking official of Nicaragua's National Development Bank, which extends credit to MIDINRA, maintained that the Ministry's "enterprises are too large to be administered well."[12] He held that there were no economies of scale in the APP. In a discussion of the conditions necessary for profitability, MIDINRA's vice-minister of economics asserted that the enterprises had to be *manejables, no monstrosos* (manageable, not monstrous).[13] Just what is manageable given the present development of administrative skills in MIDINRA—and within Nicaragua at large—is an open question. Evidence suggests, though, that the Sandinista regime has organized the state sector in a way that it does not have the capacity to manage efficiently.

Concerns about advanced technology, economies of scale, administrative capacity, and simple efficiency are especially appropriate for Nicaragua's public investments. In the first five

12. Interview with Julio Ruíz, manager of agricultural credit, National Development Bank, Managua, February 1985.

13. Meeting with Silvio Lanuza, vice-minister of economics, MIDINRA, Managua, May 1985 (cf. footnote 9; Lanuza had been promoted).

years of postrevolutionary rule, over 70 percent of the U.S.$1 billion plus allocated to investments in the public sector was concentrated in thirteen grandiose projects. While most of the capital was foreign, each of the projects entailed considerable expenditures of Nicaraguan resources. Investments managed by MIDINRA include a Cuban-built sugar mill (the largest in Central America) and two huge dairy farms. A detailed evaluation of the large state investments concurred with reports quoted earlier that the projects have "negative economic evaluations."[14] It traced difficulties not only to administrative shortcomings but also to the capital-intensive nature of the projects, the sophistication of technology employed, the dependence on imports, the cost, and the length of time to complete the projects and recoup committed capital. It found that none of the investments made a net contribution to Nicaragua's balance of payments.[15] Perhaps more important, "it is very probable that the level of public investments has affected the investment possibilities of the private sector, particularly of the peasant sector."[16]

Illustrating the limitations of state investments is MIDINRA's expensive dairy farm, Chiltepe, designed in 1981 to reduce Nicaragua's dependence on imported milk. Situated not far from Managua, the farm embraces seven thousand hectares that are eventually to support 16,800 dairy cows. It built milking stations of Cuban design, and imported sophisticated milking equipment from Sweden and dairy cattle from Canada. State controls on milk prices, however, have eroded the incentives of traditional producers. Commander Wheelock described the results:

> And the milk plants? Last week they received only 20,000 gallons of milk whereas they received 250,000 gallons a week in 1980; in other words almost no one is bringing milk to milk plants. What does this mean? That there is almost a complete erosion of prices and controls and of all the measures we have applied.[17]

14. Alejandro Argüello Huper and Nanno Kleiterp, "Inversiones 1979–1985" (Managua, 1985, Mimeographed). A synopsis of the work is published in *Pensamiento propio* 39 (February 1987), from which the quote is drawn, p. 27.
15. Ibid., p. 35.
16. Ibid., p. 30.
17. MIDINRA, *Plan de trabajo 1985* (Managua: MIDINRA, 1985), p. 18.

Price controls have also contributed to financial imbalances in the Chiltepe project. The project has many other difficulties, including the effect of Nicaragua's heat on Canadian cows. Its difficulties question the wisdom of concentrating so many resources in an enclave, especially if this strategy also neglects other producers, who are economically insignificant as individuals but important as a group.

Nicaragua's poverty of resources explains in part the disappointing performance of its state enterprises. Another factor is the pursuit of unattainable economies of scale. Yet these two alone do not explain why the Sandinistas' bid to manage the commanding heights has gone astray. They leave unanswered the question of why extant resources have often been poorly employed or diverted to activities that have no relation to the firms' business. Perhaps more central, they leave the question of why the firms are not managed as conventional firms, where everyone from laborers to the director works single-mindedly to produce a good or service, where their success determines their collective and individual well-being—as well as the survival of the firm.

## Political Responsibilities

A revealing description of the function of the agrarian state enterprises was published in a MIDINRA newsletter:

> The agrarian reform enterprises have come to play an important role in sustaining production, considered as an arm of the state in production. . . . They also act as a social and political force in economic and military tasks.[18]

An integral, if not decisive, explanation for the APP's financial losses is that firms do act as "social and political" forces. A searching internal MIDINRA report asserted that state enterprises' "elevated inefficiency is in part owing to the economic policies directed toward these enterprises."[19] But it found that

18. *Informaciones agropecuarias,* March–April 1987, p. 5.
19. MIDINRA, "Los problemas de fondo en el manejo reciente de la política agropecuaria" (Managua, 1982, Mimeographed), p. 2.

economic policies were not formulated and implemented solely on economic criteria:

> If economic policy establishes the correct relation between politics and economics, noticeable imbalances can be observed: whereas certain policies appear to be controlled directly by political crite-ria . . . others appear to be tied more to economic considerations.[20]

> The analysis suggests that agricultural policy—an aggregate of different measures—will necessarily be in conflict with "produc-tion" tendencies that favor production as an end in itself, and with "political" tendencies that favor social organization and its effect over the correlation of forces. . . . The complexity of rela-tions . . . makes a neat integration impossible.[21]

Politically inspired impositions on state firms have caused them to assume diverse responsibilities at considerable cost.

The call for state enterprises to participate in political tasks has not been clearly or uniformly articulated, partly because the call does not come from one "voice." Many spokesmen of the revolution make claims: assorted ministries, the FSLN itself, the army, the bank, unions, and neighborhood defense communities, to name but the most prominent. The inevitable ambiguity is explained in an internal MIDINRA document:

> The easiest interpretation would be to affirm that there coexist, within the same state, diverse strategies with respect to the social models they have as a point of reference; the time they have programmed for the revolutionary transformation or for an appre-ciation of the objective and social conditions, present and poten-tial; and the necessary result, in so many policies and areas of action, [is] a collection of partially contradictory policies. The result of this is the absence of a common strategy.[22]

Understandable as the multitude of claimants may be, it engenders considerable disruption within the APP. There are many demands; they are presented at different times, with varying intensity, and

20. Ibid.
21. Ibid., p. 24.
22. MIDINRA, "Conceptos básicos que guiarán la elaboración del diagnós-tico sobre estrategias y políticas del sector agropecuario" (Managua, 1982, Mim-eographed), p. 10.

frequently conflict with one another. They sap not only firms' resources but also their sense of purpose and direction.

One of the most common demands upon agrarian enterprises is to provide employment, even when their economic resources do not warrant it. One study suggests that employment in state agrarian enterprises increased 25 percent within two years of their being confiscated.[23] Demands were made not only to expand the total number of laborers but also to provide continual employment to seasonal workers, especially those on coffee and sugar estates. The emergence of labor shortages has moderated demands for employment, but MIDINRA Central recognizes that overstaffing contributes to enterprises' financial losses. Yet it explains that certain particularly unprofitable enterprises continue because they are "the only source of employment in the area."[24] And throughout MIDINRA there is a conviction that redundant workers cannot be dismissed. The motives for providing employment when there is no economic rationale encompass a genuine concern for the rural poor and a bid for their allegiance to the revolution, especially crucial in zones of counterrevolutionary activity.

The provision of employment has accompanied efforts to improve the often miserable working conditions of rural laborers. An internal MIDINRA document on the enterprises' performance traced part of their initial financial difficulties.

They had to make extensive investments and social expenditures in housing, kitchens, health centers, schools, and so forth, with the intent of improving the deplorable living conditions inherited from *somocismo*.[25]

Although the intent was to provide better conditions for laborers, in practice the local community at large often enjoyed the benefits

23. International Fund for Agricultural Development (IFAD), "Informe de la misión especial de programación a Nicaragua" (Rome, 1980, Mimeographed), p. 88.

24. Interview with Mario Alemán, administrator, MIDINRA Central, Managua, January 1985.

25. MIDINRA, "Revisión integral de las empresas estatales agropecuarias y fortalecimiento de sus sistemas de dirección y gestión" (Managua, n.d., Mimeographed), p. 142.

provided. By its third year, the postrevolutionary state scaled back "social investments." But Nicaragua continues efforts to improve what is sometimes called "social income." At some enterprises this includes transportation; at others it means hearty meals. At the Chiltepe dairy farm it involves the daily gift of a liter of milk. At other enterprises there is nothing. Mismanagement has distributed benefits unevenly and, in many instances, diluted the benefits of expensive investments and expenditures.

The cost of "social" investments and expenditures cannot be measured because of the imprecision of enterprises' accounting data. Commonly, enterprises list in their balances some investments that prove to be social expenditures. Acknowledging them as such has negative repercussions for already unfavorable annual income statements. Unsystematic but persuasive evidence suggests that attempts to improve working conditions have entailed considerable though unevenly distributed cost. Like the provision of employment, efforts to improve working conditions stem in part from heartfelt concern for the poor. And in part they respond to demands from the poor. But expenditures are motivated also by the desire to win the political allegiance of the rural majority.

In discussing the agrarian reform, an internal MIDINRA report suggests the desire for political support.

> From a political perspective, it signifies the massive incorporation into the revolutionary process of the poorest peasants, accelerating the process of conscious formation and mobilization.[26]

The common assumption at least throughout MIDINRA Central is that the rural "proletariat" employed on state farms should be even more loyal to the revolution than peasants who have received land. The state's laborers have benefited not only from the largesse of the APP but also from greater access to information about the revolution and its aims. The state does not desire the allegiance of rural laborers and peasants for vanity's sake. The FSLN has powerful enemies in rural Nicaragua—landlords, traders, and, above all, counterrevolutionaries. The Sandinistas' sur-

---

26. MIDINRA, "La política para los pequeños productores y para el semi-proletariado" (Managua, 1982, Mimeographed), p. 21.

vival depends on checking these enemies, an easier task if the rural poor are committed, or at least neutral, to the revolution.

Agrarian state enterprises have contributed directly to defense of the revolution—at considerable cost. Enterprises in border areas, like the Commander Marcos Somarriba, station troops, often giving them food, lodging, and other necessities; they also commonly provide transportation or lend vehicles. A more widespread burden is the maintenance of militias (sometimes with compulsory membership for employees) and of salaries for those employees who are called for active duty. With the latter there is not only a direct but sometimes an indirect cost of doing without trained and experienced employees. A more immediate cost is that state enterprises within reach of the counterrevolution have been attacked, whether or not they were posting soldiers. In some enterprises damage has been extensive. The bulk of MIDINRA's enterprises are, however, in the populous Pacific zone that has been free of fighting.

As with "social" investments and expenditures, defense costs have not been adequately recorded. MIDINRA, and other ministries too, regularly ask for information about damage inflicted by the counterrevolution. But the enterprises do not usually enter these costs in their accounts. Just as livestock stolen from the Enterprise Commander Marcos Somarriba does not figure in the books, so similar incidents elsewhere remain unrecorded. The state enterprises do not regularly prepare balance sheets, which would detail any changes in assets and liabilities. Only with difficulty do the firms prepare income statements that highlight financial transactions. Consequently, although the counterrevolution—as well as defense against it—has made an enormous impact on postrevolutionary Nicaragua, it does not explain the APP's poor financial performance. Still, indirect and poorly recorded as they are, defense expenditures must be reckoned as yet another burden.

A different political task performed by state enterprises is control of prices. The Sandinista regime controls the prices of most agricultural products: for agroexports controls "stabilize" the earnings of producers, and for many food commodities they work in "defense of the consumer." For both kinds of products, state-set prices have been well below those that would prevail in an unfettered market. The depressed prices are problematic because in the private sector they have undermined incentives to produce and because in the APP they have contributed to financial losses. The government has publicly acknowledged the problem and with great fanfare periodically raises selling prices. But the increases in prices always lag behind increases in production costs.[27]

For agroexport commodities there exists no alternative market for either private or state producers than state monopsonies. But private producers can sometimes adopt such defensive strategies as switching crops or slashing costs (even to the point of sacrifices in yields). Cotton producers in particular, who generated considerable foreign exchange before the revolution, have resorted to these two strategies. For food commodities, parallel and "black" markets have appeared, where private producers can usually obtain much higher prices than those the state pays. Except in extenuating circumstances, state enterprises have been prohibited from selling to anyone except the state. The sales by state enterprises have contributed to the government's efforts to moderate inflation and, more specifically, to provide essential foodstuffs at prices acceptable to poor consumers.

Fulfilling this public service has an acknowledged financial cost for state enterprises, as an internal MIDINRA report stated:

> Since their origin, the enterprises have fulfilled the role of . . . price regulators. . . . The enterprises of the APP confront a different situation than private enterprises concerning commercialization, in that the latter sell their products in the market, free or parallel; in contrast the APP enterprises have to submit their products to state organs, which pay official prices. It can be said that they take advantage of the obligatory position of the enterprises.[28]

The report went on to estimate that prevailing prices (for food commodities) in the parallel market were higher than state-paid prices by margins ranging from 25 to 300 percent.[29] Administrators of state enterprises, such as those of Oscar Turcios, often

27. MIDINRA, *Plan de trabajo 1985*, pp. 16–19.
28. MIDINRA, "Problemática de las empresas del sector agropecuario adscritas al MIDINRA," p. 7.
29. Ibid., p. 8.

argue that their losses result in large measure from low prices they receive from the state. They hold that the grossly overvalued córdoba undercuts the government's claim that it pays international prices for export crops. And MIDINRA recognizes that prices of food crops are controlled to protect consumers, in what is often explained as a "political reason."

Like costs incurred in defense of the revolution, controlled prices impose a burden that is impossible to measure. It certainly is a cost and, as such, another explanation for the financial losses of the APP. But price distortions are widespread and uneven or, as MIDINRA's Vice-Minister of Economics bluntly said, "*los precios son una locura* (prices are crazy)."[30] Inputs, including those that are imported, are also well below market prices. For example, a gallon of gasoline—imported—long cost less than two tortillas. Consideration of how state enterprises have been adversely affected by price distortions should be balanced with an appreciation of how they have benefited from these distortions. State enterprises have been net losers but not to the extent their administrators claim.

In addition to fulfilling these significant tasks, state enterprises have made other contributions to the revolution, or the "process" as cadres often refer to it. To assist the agrarian reform, state enterprises have ceded land and capital to cooperatives. Usually the land and capital are not central to the enterprises' activities, but firms commonly retain the debt corresponding to the donated land parcels.[31] The Enterprise Commander Marcos Somarriba was asked to host, and underwrite, an expensive vegetable-growing project. Other contributions abound: entertaining visiting dignitaries, ferrying people to demonstrations, even lending trucks to the local Committee for Sandinista Defense (CDS) to haul away garbage.[32] These and similar activities have a cost.

Another political use of state enterprises does not inflict a cost upon them. State enterprises serve to caution—or to threaten—

30. Meeting with Silvio Lanuza, vice-minister of economics, MIDINRA, Managua, May 1985.

31. MIDINRA, "Revisión integral de las empresas estatales agropecuarias," p. 143.

32. Interview with Roger Fonseca, manager of the UPE Tierras Blancas, the Enterprise Oscar Benavides, Chagüitillo Sébaco, May 1985.

the private sector: any private businesses that thwart the revolution can be absorbed by a state enterprise. A much discussed example involved the leader of the principal private sector organization, the Superior Council of Private Enterprise (COSEP). Enrique Bolaños began to engage in spirited public pronouncements against the revolution. His cotton estate was confiscated, nominally because it was needed to provide land to peasants. But the estate was taken over by the Enterprise Camilo Ortega, and the private sector reached the desired conclusion: engaging in political opposition can lead to the loss of one's assets.[33] More commonly, private enterprises are confiscated because of inactivity or even decapitalization. While retaining a commitment to "national unity," the Sandinista regime has let the private sector know that it will not tolerate vitriolic public criticism and that private capital must be used fully and efficiently. State enterprises help enforce these mandates.

With the multiple political tasks routinely fulfilled by the agrarian state enterprises, it is not surprising that more than one internal MIDINRA report has complained that the enterprises are viewed as "the 'state' and not as 'producer.' "[34] And it is understandable that a ranking Nicaraguan banker, who oversees MIDINRA's portfolio, laments, "the concept of a firm has been lost."[35]

> There is a duality in the treatment of the enterprises; they are viewed as being the state in some cases . . . in other cases they are viewed as being like any other producer. Roles so contradictory and incompatible confound and obscure the fundamental objective of the enterprises, which is to produce at the lowest cost.[36]

The ambiguous conception of state enterprises, with its economic repercussions, does not result only from the firms' methodical pursuit of political objectives that the Sandinista leadership ordered. That is part of the explanation. The conception of the

33. *Barricada,* 29 June 1985.
34. For example, MIDINRA, "Sistema de dirección de empresas," p. 2.
35. Interview with Antonio Medrano, administrator, Bank of America, Managua, February 1985.
36. MIDINRA, "Problemática de las empresas del sector agropecuario adscritas al MIDINRA," p. 9.

enterprises as the "state" is also based on a new mentalité ushered in by the revolution. This mentalité has, among other consequences, led to a widespread discarding of the traditional concept of the firm and complicated the management of Nicaragua's commanding heights.

## The Revolutionary Mentalité

The insurrection that culminated in the ouster of Somoza also assaulted the values and norms of his regime. It and the economic system that underpinned it were denounced as unjust and exploitative. Agitation deepened the people's sense of deprivation and created hope for a better future. The implicit suggestion of revolutionary rhetoric was that a better life was possible for Nicaraguans, but that the rapaciousness of the Somoza regime had choked it off. The triumph of the revolution unleashed a widespread euphoria and a belief that unfulfilled needs would finally be met. Many poor Nicaraguans thought that after the revolution they would suddenly have everything they had never had before; they would no longer have to work. Everything associated with the old regime was discredited.

These sentiments together can be loosely called a revolutionary mentalité, whose politically charged impact is difficult to delineate, let alone measure. But in the aftermath of the revolution there has most certainly been a consequential change in attitudes toward work and authority. On the positive side, the revolutionary mentalité has given the Sandinista leadership and its cadres a sense of purpose, a willingness to act, a disregard for risk, and an indifference to personal hardship. However, the revolutionary mentalité has brought unexpected difficulties that contribute to postrevolutionary Nicaragua's vexatious managerial environment. These difficulties include an abrupt drop in the productivity of laborers, ambiguity about the objectives of economic entities, a slighting of traditional managerial practices, and disrespect for economic—in contrast to political—locuses of authority (for example, banks). These difficulties are consequential in their own right. And, because they undermine economic rationality, they have encouraged the already existing proclivity to use economic entities for political tasks.

Since they came to power, the Sandinista leaders have acknowledged that revolutionary aspirations have to be tempered and that certain facile, self-serving interpretations of the revolution are misleading. The Sandinistas' own rhetoric has slowly but surely changed, for example, from inciting workers' militancy to pleading for laborers' productivity. But the Sandinistas' enduring convictions, the danger of frustrating popular aspirations they themselves created, and the presence of counterrevolutionaries prevent the Sandinistas from tackling problematic dimensions of the revolutionary mentalité. With cynics and counterrevolutionaries present, they must accommodate even reckless and lax followers. There are gingerly worded admonishments, weak incentives, and no sanctions. The underlying dilemma involves an often ugly trade-off between financial responsibility and political sensitivity. Economic and political logics clash.

Peasants' and rural laborers' interpretation of the revolution has been especially problematic, presenting the Sandinista regime with a tremendous fall in labor productivity. Peasants and rural laborers were most likely to believe that the triumph of the revolution meant they would have everything they never had and would no longer have to work. For the rural poor suddenly to "have everything" proved impossible, however: there were few liquid assets to seize and redistribute. Rural Nicaragua is poor, and its productive facilities cannot quickly be turned into household goods. Although frustrated in their naive desire for sudden luxury, the rural poor proved more successful in achieving the second part of their expectation, "that they no longer have to work."[37]

Rural laborers throughout Nicaragua spontaneously took advantage of the near anarchy in the countryside to reduce dramatically their labor obligations. Those employed for daily wages simply cut back on the length of the working day. Those employed for piece-rate work (*tareas*) insisted on switching to daily

37. The nuances of the behavior of peasants and rural laborers are explored in Forrest D. Colburn, "Foot Dragging and Other Peasant Responses to the Nicaraguan Revolution," *Peasant Studies* 13 (Winter 1986): 77–96.

wages and then followed their brethren in shortening their working day. Rural laborers working for the private sector were able to reduce the hours they worked partly because economic activity slowed during the insurrection; apprehensive employers tolerated their shorter working hours and greater laxity. The revolution irrevocably altered traditional patrón-worker relations.

The state was more affected than the private sector by the labor militancy the FSLN fostered. Hours worked per day on newly established state enterprises fell nearly everywhere. And state enterprises found themselves pressured into increasing employment, usually above what was necessary. An internal MIDINRA report described rural laborers' attitude:

> The peasant has come to see the new proprietor as "state" and not as "producer" and thus his expectations, rather than to exchange his efforts with this new producer, are instead to ask and often to demand from it as the state, even before the generation of some kind of surplus, the social benefits that he had been deprived under the previous form of exploitation.[38]

Another internal MIDINRA report complained that Sandinista-fostered unions exacerbated the fall in labor productivity.

> The union organization in the countryside is strongest in state enterprises and has not reached the level of maturity that the workers potentially have and to the contrary has caused a fall in the productivity of labor and a decline in labor discipline.[39]

Many administrators of state enterprises maintain that their most difficult and intractable problem is labor indiscipline.

Nicaraguans' class perspective makes the spontaneous pursuit of reduced labor obligations eminently rational. The fundamental maxim of economic logic, that people desire more rather than less, has a corollary: in exchange for what they desire people likewise offer less rather than more. Rural poor Nicaraguans, frustrated in their desire for an immediate improvement in their standard of living, simply took their "historical vacation." How-

---

38. MIDINRA, "Problemática de las empresas del sector agropecuario adscritas al MIDINRA," p. 3.
39. MIDINRA, "Sistema de dirección de empresas," p. 3.

ever, this rational strategy exacerbated the new regime's financial difficulties and complicated its relations with labor.

The difficulties that rural laborers present to the revolutionary regime are openly acknowledged and regularly reported—for example, in *Barricada,* the state newspaper. Commander Wheelock summarized the problem:

> Since the triumph of the revolution we have observed in the countryside that contracts made by labor organizations with the Ministry of Labor, and in general with productive enterprises, have presented a tendency to set lower norms for work than existed previously. In sugar, the fall has equaled 40 percent of the historic norm, in rice 25 percent, in coffee 60 percent, this is to say, a very steep fall in the productivity of labor. What has happened as a consequence of this? Now we need two workers to do what one did before.[40]

The problem of low productivity is augmented by "a lack of discipline" that "complicates the management of state enterprises."[41] Workers make demands; and "if expectations are not met they feel frustrated and cynical."[42]

MIDINRA has carefully attempted to restore labor discipline and productivity. Moral suasion is used to convince rural laborers of the Sandinistas' commitment to their welfare and of the very real constraints, such as the counterrevolution, on governmental resources. But many appeals, like the posting of signs proclaiming, "production is revolutionary," are too wooden to convince peasants. More important, declining real incomes retard the state's efforts to reverse the decline in labor productivity. A UPE manager at the Enterprise Oscar Turcios summarized the changing responses peasants made when exhorted to increase productivity: "After the Revolution they said, 'No, we are free.' Now they say, 'You are too demanding; the salary is very low.' "[43]

---

40. Wheelock, *Entre la crisis y la agresión,* p. 110.
41. Interview with Manuel Castro and Fidel Olivas, administrators, office of MIDINRA's fourth region, Estelí, January 1985.
42. Ibid.
43. Interview with Santo López, manager of a UPE, the Enterprise Oscar Turcios, Estelí, February 1985.

In an effort to reverse the decline in labor productivity, MIDINRA began a campaign during the 1984–1985 agricultural season to provide monetary incentives for laborers to work for piece-rate earnings instead of daily wages.[44] The approach, called *normalización* (the setting of work norms), was copied from Cuba, where it has proven effective in increasing workers' productivity.[45] Preliminary results show that Nicaraguan laborers have responded favorably to the setting of work norms.[46] They often earn additional income at the same time that state enterprises reduce costs. Despite the gains in productivity, more of which are expected, the legacy of labor indiscipline suggests that the very values that revolutionaries preach—and that help them gain power—subsequently erode the state's capacity to manage the commanding heights of the economy.

The revolutionary mentalité of administrators also contributes to the financial woes of the agrarian APP, although less visibly. Administrators have not interpreted the revolution as meaning the end of toil. On the contrary, they tend to work hard. But they concentrate their efforts on producing goods and services with little, if any, thought to the cost or the net economic consequences of their activities. Their indifference may come from their training; many administrators are agricultural technicians. And simply attending to the day-to-day obstacles of the field or shop floor is daunting. However, the indifference to financial details also reflects administrators' common attitude that they are working in the service of the revolution. Other than self-aggrandizement, which is rare, whatever they do is justified—and deserves others' cooperation. "Control" is unnecessary because they are the state, the revolution.

The problem in state enterprises is not just that systems of planning, accounting, and control may be poorly designed and implemented but that they also receive inadequate attention. The

44. MIDINRA, *La normación del trabajo* (Managua: MIDINRA, 1985).

45. Discussed in Central Junta of Planning, *El sistema de dirección y planificación de la economía en las empresas* (Havana: Editorial de Ciencias Sociales, 1981), pp. 123–135.

46. Interview with Panfilo Cruz, manager of the complejo El Limón, the Enterprise Oscar Benavides, Chagüitillo Sébaco, May 1985; *Barricada*, 29 July 1985, 10 April 1986.

comments of an administrator discussing the management of state enterprises in the Matagalpa region are suggestive:

> The annual plan is written at a desk; no one speaks to those in production. The plan is prepared too quickly. There is no participation, not in the formulation of the plan or in its implementation. The plan is not used. . . . Directors do not ask for information about costs. . . . Administrators of enterprises do not seem interested or concerned with the prices they receive for their goods and services, only with the amount of financing they receive.[47]

The portrait is similar to that of the Enterprise Oscar Turcios. And it is undoubtedly what an internal MIDINRA report referred to when it complained of "an ideology in the enterprises and regional offices of anti-control and anti-planning."[48]

The widespread disregard for costs is rooted in perceptions of what is important—and what is not. Particularly in contrast to the management of the Enterprise Oscar Turcios, Camilo Ortega illustrates an atypical mentalité. What is striking about the Enterprise Camilo Ortega's exemplary financial success is that so much of it seems to stem from the atypical values—and behavior—of the firm's founding director. Despite his revolutionary credentials, he managed the enterprise in a fashion true to his bourgeois background. In so doing, he clashed with the more "revolutionary" approach of his colleagues.

The dominant values held by state administrators lead them, as a whole, to laxity not only in controlling their costs and revenues but also in meeting their financial obligations. The delays engender conflict, often pitting the state against the state. Enterprises are delinquent in paying for their utilities, write checks without funds to cover them, and even fail to pay their bills to one another. Most noticeably, MIDINRA's commercial enterprises routinely delay—for months—payment to MIDINRA's production enterprises for the goods they purchase.[49] In contrast, MIDINRA's commercial entities pay private enterprises promptly.

---

47. Interview with Marta García, administrator, the Enterprise Antonio Ramírez, Matagalpa, January 1985.
48. MIDINRA, "Sistema de dirección de empresas," p. 10.
49. MIDINRA, "Relaciones comerciales entre las empresas agropecuarias adscritas a MIDINRA y a las empresas comercializadoras 1985" (Managua, 1985, Mimeographed).

Conflict is most evident and consequential in dealings with the nationalized banking system. Summing up the attitude of many administrators, one enterprise director called the bank a "monster."[50] At worst it appears as an ugly capitalist legacy and at best a bureaucracy insensitive to the needs of the revolution. Conflict abounds, but the enterprises prevail. As one administrator said, "It is always possible to receive more money from the bank, claiming that if additional funds are not received, production will be disrupted."[51] But negotiations are a "game."[52] Convincing final arguments for bankers yet unpaid to lend more money include "It will not be possible to pay the workers and then there will be a political problem."[53]

According to a senior Nicaraguan banker, the attitude of the Sandinista regime is simply that "the productive sector should have all of the privileges of the bank."[54] He recalled an incident where the director of one of MIDINRA's sugar refineries submitted a request for supplementary funds. The banker said he could not make a decision and wanted first to review the firm's accounts. The director of the enterprise told him, "Listen, you son-of-a-whore, you give us the money or I am going to come to your office with four thousand men with machetes, because you are holding up production."[55] The banker granted the loan. For him, "There is no backing from the government to act as a banker." If he does, all he gets is a "disagreeable afternoon."[56]

As the banker's comments suggest, responsibility for the prevailing managerial environment—in which it is rational for an administrator to slight economic criteria—belongs to Nicaragua's leadership. In a revealing passage, Commander Wheelock, writing more as a member of the ruling FSLN National Directorate than as minister of MIDINRA, suggests the origins of Nicara-

50. Interview with Manuel Duarte, director of the Enterprise Adolfo García Barberena, El Crucero, January 1985.
51. Interview with Alberto Gallo, administrator, the Enterprise Julio Buitrago, Masachapa, January 1985.
52. Interview with Iván Zelaya, economics director for MIDINRA's Region V, Matagalpa, January 1985.
53. Ibid.
54. Interview with Antonio Medrano, administrator, Bank of America, Managua, February 1985.
55. Ibid.
56. Ibid.

gua's managerial mentalité. In discussing Nicaragua's crisis, he acknowledges the regime has overburdened itself economically. He asks himself,

> Why? for the morale of the revolutionary to do everything. . . . It is a revolutionary attitude to defy aspects of everyday life and some economic realities.[57]

His following sentence is equally suggestive:

> Of course, after a while the Central Bank began to complain of monetary emissions. . . .[58]

Economic realities cannot be defied for long, particularly in a small, poor country.

57. Wheelock, *Entre la crisis y la agresión,* p. 74.
58. Ibid.

# 7

## State Enterprises as a Development Strategy

Ruling Sandinista comandantes attribute Nicaragua's problematic economy to a powerful set of exogenous constraints, beginning justifiably with the United States–supported counterrevolution. The counterrevolution has taken the lives of thousands of Nicaraguans. Battles have been fought far from Nicaragua's populous, and economically important, Pacific region; but the war nonetheless has a high economic cost. Resources that would have contributed to economic development have been channeled to defense. Punitive trade and credit measures by the United States have taken a toll too. Compounding the difficulties imposed by the counterrevolution was the downward turn of the world economy that rocked all the countries of Latin America and began in 1979, the year that the revolution triumphed. The prices of Nicaragua's export commodities weakened while the prices of imports held firm or even increased.

The state of the Nicaraguan economy and the visible international constraints on the regime's autonomy prompted an Argentinian commentator to conclude that in revolutionary settings like Nicaragua's, economies in the process of restructuring "are not viable." For him, the implication was clear:

Assistance from the "advanced" revolutions is essential to guarantee the initial viability of social revolutions in less-developed and highly dependent economies.[1]

Indeed, foreign donations and credits to Nicaragua, largely but not exclusively from the Soviet Union, have been decisive in enabling the Sandinista regime to survive the initial years of postrevolutionary rule. Given the strength of the counterrevolution, military aid (overwhelmingly as donations) has been essential. Credits for oil, machinery for construction and agriculture, food, and other goods have been significant. The value of foreign assistance annually exceeds the value of Nicaragua's exports by a factor of between two and three. The obverse of foreign assistance has been a rapid rise in Nicaragua's foreign debt from U.S.$1.5 billion in 1979 to U.S.$7 billion in 1987.

Although foreign assistance has been crucial to Nicaragua, it has been unable either to prevent a marked decline in the standard of living or, in itself, to provide a catalyst for sustained economic growth. The management of Nicaragua's economy remains important. Inauspiciously, the evidence presented here demonstrates trenchant limitations in the state's capacity to marshal and employ resources. The same limitations appear to bedevil other contemporary postrevolutionary regimes, such as those in Ethiopia and Mozambique. As in Nicaragua, state capacity in these countries appears to be limited not just by poverty but also by the unseen manipulation of economic enterprises for political ends and by a revolutionary mentalité that undermines economic rationality.

An analysis of Ethiopia's state enterprises presented a view, and explanation, of their performance that could well have been that of Nicaragua's enterprises:

> During a working visit . . . Chairman Mengistu . . . noted with heavy concern the shortcomings of the state farms and how the performance and operations of the state agro-industrial activities were far from desirable and at times catastrophic. He commented

1. Carlos Vilas, "Troubles Everywhere," in *The Political Economy of Revolutionary Nicaragua*, ed. Rose Spalding (Boston: Allen and Unwin, 1987), pp. 245, 246.

that following the government take-over the farms seemed to have turned into a consumption of available assets instead of producing incomes.[2]

The report traced, broadly, poor performance to politics: "Political expediency is much more important than economic rationality."[3]

In a speech the late Samora Machel offered a frank critique of Mozambique's state enterprises:

> What did we find in your factories? We saw that you produce very little. So we then asked . . . how we can increase productivity? The answer was always the same: it is impossible to raise productivity because in most enterprises there is poor time-keeping, absenteeism, liberalism, a lack of respect for institutions, confusion . . . the result is low productivity. Using the same machinery as you had in colonial times, in the same plants, with the same number of employees, and often the same technicians, you have reduced productivity![4]

Machel suggested that much of the problem derived from a mistaken political mentalité among laborers. "They abuse the leeway allowed them and when their attention is called to this, they say: 'Colonialism's finished, exploitation's over.' "[5]

The report on Ethiopia likewise suggested that prevailing interpretations of what constitutes "revolution" contribute to difficulties. Unlike Machel, though, the author focused on administrators:

> Because of . . . revolutionary zeal there is a tendency and over-enthusiasm to impress on the need to be progressive, anti-reactionary and therefore relieve oneself from the ties of all habits, customs, techniques, and functions attached to the old order, and thus a tendency for rejecting financial and accounting techniques and tools as capitalist methods not useful to the socialist setting.[6]

2. Johannes Kinfu, "Towards Understanding the Public Corporation, and/or Public Enterprise, State Enterprise in a Socialist Industrial Transformation and to Provide Proper Accounting for It," (Addis Ababa, 1980, Mimeographed), p. 25.
3. Ibid., p. 27.
4. Samora Machel, *Samora Machel* (London: Zed Press, 1985), p. 113.
5. Ibid., p. 117.
6. Johannes Kinfu, "Towards Understanding the Public Corporation," p. 27.

Again, the same argument could just as persuasively apply to Nicaragua.

The similarity among the financial performances of the state sectors of three postrevolutionary regimes—Nicaragua, Ethiopia, and Mozambique, countries otherwise quite different from one another—suggests that state management of the nationalized commanding heights proves to be a problem for postrevolutionary regimes in the poor parts of the world. Moreover, the surprise that Mengistu, Machel, and the Sandinista comandantes express at the result of state initiative implies that problems are unpredicted and therefore especially vexing. Perhaps because of confidence gained from ousting the old order, emergent revolutionary leaders exaggerate the capacities of the institutions under their command. Whatever the explanation, the broad conclusion is that postrevolutionary leaders make decisions not only under considerable pressure but without knowledge of probable outcomes.

The Nicaraguan case suggests that even if state enterprises were not plagued by inefficiency and financial loss, their isolation from the majority of rural poor and their economic activities would still constrain their contribution to rural Nicaragua. Revolutionary regimes are not responsible for the unequal distribution of productive capital they inherit. But to build on prevailing inequalities through channeling scarce resources to the "commanding heights" of the economy may be unwise. In Nicaragua, and seemingly also in Ethiopia and Mozambique, state enterprises and investments have the quality of enclaves. An internal MIDINRA report admitted as much:

> Ordinarily, once constituted the enterprises began to function with their own economic rationality, frequently in a manner similar to an enclave with very little relation to the productive activity of the surrounding environment.[7]

For example, the justification for the expensive Chiltepe dairy farm is a shortage of milk stemming from the low yields of traditional producers, a liter and a half daily per cow. Building a

7. Ministry of Agricultural Development and Agrarian Reform (MIDINRA), "Revisión integral de las empresas estatales agropecuarias y fortalecimiento de sus sistemas de dirección y gestión" (Managua, n.d., Mimeographed), p. 145.

state-of-the-art dairy farm, with yields of up to sixteen liters, will—if difficulties can be surmounted—augment production.[8] But the investment does nothing to improve the productivity or welfare of the thousands of traditional milk producers. Similar examples abound. Furthermore, reliance on state enterprises as the axis of production likely perpetuates hierarchical relations of management because of enterprises' size and employment of more sophisticated technology.

Although questions can be raised about the potential contribution of state enterprises to equitable development, the more immediate concern for hard-pressed governors and administrators is the financial performance of what is usually a significant part of the economy. Seemingly inevitable financial losses, with their multifaceted repercussions, prompt a search for reform.

In postrevolutionary regimes the impetus for reform of state enterprises is circumscribed by the same forces that necessitate reform. First, the resources to contemplate and experiment with reforms are often lacking. Second, revolutionary authority may face continued challenges, which it can check in part by a prominent role in the economy. Third, the employment of economic entities to fulfill political tasks often generates a constituency, whose new advantages are often difficult to withdraw. Fourth, the continued necessity of appearing "revolutionary," of distancing itself from the old order, constrains the regime's possibilities of reform, including the idea of jettisoning state enterprises altogether. Individually and collectively, the last three explanations suggest the mean trade-off between political benefits and economic costs.

These constraints often mean, as in Nicaragua, that reform is limited to discussions of petty details. Excluded are consequential issues such as a clear definition of the objectives of enterprises, and of their relations to party, bureaucracy, and citizen. At least in the case of Nicaragua, these more fundamental issues have been either ignored or, more commonly, ambiguously treated. For example, less than three months after Commander Wheelock publicly proclaimed that all Nicaragua's state enter-

8. Jaime Wheelock, *Entre la crisis y la agresión* (Managua: MIDINRA, 1984), p. 51.

prises must be profitable or they would be shut down, he told a group of enterprise directors completing a seminar on administration, "The technical study of administration is important, but it is necessary to have revolutionary solutions to the problems of the enterprises."[9] The APP has to have "historical content."[10]

The difficulty of restoring economic rationality in the workplace is compounded by the issue of incentives, of providing stimulus to administrators and laborers. Speaking to the gathered directors, Commander Wheelock asserted that incentives are the central problem of Nicaragua's state enterprises. He said, "Capitalism has resolved the problem of incentives, but we have not found it. . . . We have nationalized the land, but we have not nationalized the consciousness."[11] The inability to nationalize the consciousness leaves resort to punishment and reward. But they are both distasteful to revolutionary leaders. An Ethiopian report quoted Lenin as saying that managers should be punished with long prison sentences if they did not succeed in operating at a profit.[12] But state employees are political comrades, especially in the presence of a counterrevolution. Loyalty is important and cannot be jeopardized. Obversely, rewards of any kind hark back to capitalism. In short, politics is paramount not only in effecting problems in the management of state enterprises but also in thwarting their solution.

## In Fine

The difficulties of extracting state enterprises from their inevitable financial losses suggest that revolutionaries and their sympathizers must weigh their conviction of the value of nationalization and state management of dominant economic entities. The need for this reassessment is augmented by the erosion of support for the regime that accompanies the state enterprises'

9. Speech by Commander Jaime Wheelock, minister of MIDINRA, Managua, May 1985.

10. Ibid.

11. Ibid.

12. Johannes Kinfu, "Towards Understanding the Public Corporation," p. 15.

continued inefficiency. Aspirations for social change and distaste for private property and initiative need to be paired with a sober calculation of state capacity.

Revolutionary leaders cannot escape the necessity of pursuing an economic program that leads to growth or at least does not diminish capital stock and the output of goods and services. Yet it is facile to suggest that economic policies be designed without consideration of a postrevolutionary regime's political aspirations and needs. There is a positive relation, however, between radical policies that bring considerable disruption—and hostility—and work to keep the support of groups who can check "enemies of the revolution." Moderate economic policies occasion less political strife—and thus need fewer political resources. The calibration of political and economic change must be made in tandem.

The course and sustenance of revolution are decided by the resolution of many issues, but perhaps most important are the questions of the ownership and the organization of the work place, be it farm or factory. The demonstrated preference of postrevolutionary elites is for state ownership in the most important sectors of the economy. There are compelling reasons for electing to employ state enterprises in the bid to build a more equitable society. One must realize, however, that nationalization itself brings no cornucopia of resources. Indeed, evidence suggests it brings a host of risks. Nationalization may stop the squandering of profit margins on frivolous luxuries. But care must be taken to ensure that profit margins are not absorbed by burgeoning bureaucracies or do not disappear altogether through slovenly administration and worker indiscipline. For state enterprises to contribute to a country's development, this potential benefit must be recognized as requiring the mundane traits of successful private enterprises—efficiency, innovation, and investment. This recognition depends in turn on revolutionary leaders, and their followers, appreciating that nationalized firms are not the local branch of a munificent and benevolent government.

# Bibliography

Academy of Science of the USSR. Contemporary Social Sciences. *Nicaragua: Glorioso camino a la victoria*. Moscow: Academy of Science of the USSR, 1982.

Acosta Santana, José. *Teoría y práctica de los mecanismos de dirección de la economía en Cuba*. Havana: Editorial de Ciencias Sociales, 1983.

Arce, Bayardo. *Romper la dependencia: Tarea estratégica de la revolución*. Managua: National Secretariat of Propaganda and Public Education of the FSLN, 1980.

Argüello, Alejandro, Edwin Croes, and Nanno Kleiterp. "Inversiones en Nicaragua: Logros y dificultades." *Pensamiento propio* 39 (February 1987): 21–36.

Argüello Hüper, Alejandro, and Nanno Kleiterp. "Inversiones 1979–1985." Managua, 1985. Mimeographed.

Austin, James, and John Ickis. "Management, Managers and Revolution." *World Development* 14 (1986): 775–790.

Bakhash, Shaul. *The Reign of the Ayatollahs: Iran and the Islamic Revolution*. New York: Basic Books, 1984.

Barahona, Amaru, Amalia Chamorro, Alberto Lanuza, and Juan Luis Vásquez. *Economía y sociedad en la construcción del estado en Nicaragua*. San Jose: ICAP, 1983.

Barahona Saénz, Manuel. "La productividad del trabajo y la normación en el tabaco." Managua, 1985. Mimeographed.

Baumeister, Eduardo, and Oscar Neira Cuadra. "Iniciativas de desarrollo y política en la transición sandinista." Managua, n.d. Mimeographed.

———. "The Making of a Mixed Economy: Class Struggle and State Policy in the Nicaraguan Transition." In *Transition and Development: Problems of Third World Socialism*, edited by Richard R.

137

Fagen, Carmen Diana Deere, and José Luis Coraggio, pp. 171–191. New York: Monthly Review Press, 1986.

Berrís, Rubén, and Marc Edelman. "Los vínculos económicos de Nicaragua con los países socialistas." *Comercio exterior* 10 (October 1985): 998–1006.

Boholavsky, Abel. "Relaciones laborales, condiciones de trabajo, salud ocupacional y cambio social." Managua, 1985. Mimeographed.

Brundenius, Claes. *Estrategia del desarrollo industrial en Nicaragua: 1979–1984*. Managua: CRIES, 1985.

Cabieses, Hugo. "Notas sobre la crisis económica de Nicaragua 1979–1986." Managua, 1986. Mimeographed.

Casas, Joseph. *La Stratégie agroalimentaire de Cuba depuis 1959 et ses résultats*. Montpellier: Centre de recherches agronomiques INRA, 1985.

Castañeda, Jorge. *Nicaragua: Contradicciones en la revolución*. Mexico City: Editores Tiempo Extra, 1980.

Center for the Study of Agrarian Reform. (CIERA). *Lunes socioeconómico de Barricada*. Managua: MIDINRA, 1984.

Central American Institute of Public Administration (ICAP). "Las empresas públicas y otros organismos descentralizados en la república de Nicaragua." San Jose, 1978. Mimeographed.

Central American University (UCA). Department of Sociology. "Poder popular en Nicaragua: Hacia una caracterización del estado sandinista." In *La crisis centroamericana,* edited by Daniel Camacho and Manuel Rojas, pp. 381–400. San Jose: Editorial Universitaria Centroamericana, 1984.

Central Bank of Nicaragua. "Clasificación y políticas de financiamiento de empresas MIDINRA." Managua, 1984. Mimeographed.

———. "Normas monetarias." Managua, 1986. Mimeographed.

———. "Síntesis de las principales leyes y decretos sobre política fiscal promulgados entre 1979 y 1983." Managua, 1984. Mimeographed.

Central Junta of Planning. *El sistema de dirección y planificación de la economía en las empresas*. Havana: Editorial de Ciencias Sociales, 1981.

Cibotti, Ricardo, and Enrique Sierra. *El sector público en la planificación del desarrollo*. Mexico City: Siglo Veintiuno Editores, 1984.

Colburn, Forrest D. "Foot Dragging and Other Peasant Responses to the Nicaraguan Revolution." *Peasant Studies* 13 (Winter 1986): 77–96.

———. *Post-Revolutionary Nicaragua: State, Class, and the Dilemmas of Agrarian Policy*. Berkeley: University of California Press, 1986.

Consulting Advisers of the USSR Gosplan. "Considerations on the Economic Policy of Ethiopia for the Next Few Years." Addis Ababa, 1985. Mimeographed.

Davydov, Vladimir. "Base objetiva de las transformaciones económico-sociales." In *La revolución en Nicaragua: Ayer y hoy*, edited by Alexandr Sujostat, pp. 111–120. Moscow: Editorial Progreso, 1985.

Delgado, Rodolfo. "Sobre las medidas de ajuste y la crisis económica de Nicaragua." Managua, 1985. Mimeographed.

Economic Commission for Latin America and the Caribbean (CEPAL). *La evolución de la economía de América Latina en 1986*. Santiago: CEPAL, 1988.

Elster, John. *Explaining Technical Change*. Cambridge: Cambridge University Press, 1983.

Enterprise Camilo Ortega. "Plan técnico." Masaya, 1984. Mimeographed.

Enterprise Commander Marcos Somarriba, "Estados financieros ciclo 1983–1984." San Carlos, 1984. Mimeographed.

Figueroa Aguilar, Luis Enrique. "El papel del estado en la revolución popular sandinista." Managua, 1983. Mimeographed.

Gallardo, María Eugenia, and José Roberto López. *La crisis en cifras*. San Jose: IICA-FLACSO, 1986.

Galvez, Carlos Manuel. "El estado y clases sociales en Nicaragua." Managua, 1981. Mimeographed.

García, Evaristo. "Anotaciones en torno a la política de precios de los principales productos agropecuarios en Nicaragua." Managua, 1985. Mimeographed.

González Rodríguez, Lázaro. La introducción de los principios básicos de la organización científica del trabajo en la economía cubana. Havana: Editorial de Ciencias Sociales, 1977.

Griffin, Keith, and Roger Hay. "Problems of Agricultural Development in Socialist Ethiopia: An Overview and a Suggested Strategy." *Journal of Peasant Studies* 13 (1985): 37–66.

Hanlon, Joseph. *Mozambique: The Revolution Under Fire*. London: Zed Press, 1984.

Helms, Mary. "The Society and its Environment." In *Nicaragua: A Country Study*, edited by James Rudolph, pp. 61–101. Washington, D.C.: Department of the Army, U.S. Government, 1981.

*Inforpress*, 1983, 1984, 1985, 1986, 1987.

Institute for National Development (INFONAC). *Posición competitiva del tabaco tipo habano producido en Nicaragua con respecto al mercado norteamericano*. Managua: INFONAC, 1967.

———. *Programa Trienal de desarrollo tabacalero*. Managua: INFONAC, 1966.

International Fund for Agricultural Development (IFAD). "Informe de la misión especial de programación a Nicaragua." Rome, 1980. Mimeographed.

Johannes Kinfu. "Towards Understanding the Public Corporation, and/ or Public Enterprise, State Enterprise in a Socialist Industrial Transformation and to Provide Proper Accounting for It." Addis Ababa, 1980. Mimeographed.

Kirichenko, V. *La planificación a largo plazo de la economía socialista.* Moscow: Editorial Progreso, 1981.

Komin, Anatoli N. *Cuestiones de la formación de precios planificados.* Havana: Editorial de Ciencias Sociales, 1985.

Krueger, Walter, and James E. Austin. *Organization and Control of Agricultural State-Owned Enterprises: The Case of Nicaragua.* Working Paper no. 19, Graduate School of Business Administration, Harvard University. Cambridge, Mass.: Harvard University Press, 1983.

Latin American Center of Development Administration (CLAD). *Gobierno y empresas públicas en América Latina.* Buenos Aires: Ediciones SIAP, 1978.

Leikun Berhanu. "The Management of Industrial Enterprises in Ethiopia." Addis Ababa, 1986. Mimeographed.

Lozano, Lucrecia. "Los albores de la revolución." In *Centroamérica: Una historia sin retoque,* edited by Instituto de investigaciones económicas, UNAM, pp. 245–294. Mexico City: El Día en Libros, 1987.

MacEwan, Arthur. *Revolution and Economic Development in Cuba.* New York: St. Martin's Press, 1981.

Machel, Samora. *Samora Machel: An African Revolutionary.* London: Zed Press, 1985.

Martell, Raúl. *La empresa socialista.* Havana: Editorial de Ciencias Sociales, 1979.

Martínez, Jorge Detrinidad. *Diccionario de contabilidad.* Managua: Ediciones Monimbo, 1982.

———. *Diccionario de contabilidad.* Managua: Ediciones Monimbo, 1986.

———. *Glosario socio-económico.* Managua: Ediciones Monimbo, 1983.

Marzal, Antonio. "Empresa y democracia económica." Managua, 1983. Mimeographed.

Maydanik, Kiva. "La unidad: Un problema clave." In *La revolución en Nicaragua: Ayer y hoy,* edited by Alexandr Sujostat, pp. 100–110. Moscow: Editorial Progreso, 1985.

Medal, José Luis. "Las crisis y las políticas macroeconómicas." Managua, 1986. Mimeographed.

———. *La revolución nicaragüense: Balance económico y alternativas futuras.* Managua: Ediciones Nicaragua Hoy, 1985.

———. "Políticas de estabilización y ajuste estructural en Nicaragua (1980–1986)." San Jose, 1987. Mimeographed.

Mesa-Lago, Carmelo. *The Economy of Socialist Cuba: A Two-Decade Appraisal.* Albuquerque: University of New Mexico Press, 1981.

Mikoyán, Sergó "Las enseñanzas de la revolución en Nicaragua desde el punto de vista de la teoría y la práctica del movimiento libertador." In *La revolución en Nicaragua: Ayer y hoy,* edited by Alexandr Sujostat, pp. 73–86. Moscow: Editorial Progreso, 1985.

Ministry of Agricultural Development and Agrarian Reform (MIDINRA). "Acerca del problema de la competencia entre metas para diversos cultivos." Managua, 1982. Mimeographed.

———. "Actividades a desarrollar por la división de organización y gestión empresarial y balance de recursos humanos y materiales." Managua, 1985. Mimeographed.

———. "Administración de empresas estatales: El caso de Nicaragua, aspecto financiero." Managua, 1985. Mimeographed.

———. "Comisión y análisis financiero: empresas de reforma agraria." Managua, 1985. Mimeographed.

———. "Conceptos básicos que guiarán la elaboración del diagnóstico sobre estrategias y políticas del sector agropecuario." Managua, 1982. Mimeographed.

———. *La dirección nacional y la organización campesina.* Managua: Ediciones Tierra Arada, 1986.

———. "Directorio." Managua, 1984. Mimeographed.

———. "Enfoque de la situación coyuntural de los mataderos estatales." Managua, 1981. Mimeographed.

———. "Evaluación financiera de las empresas de reforma agraria ciclo 1983–1984." Managua, 1984. Mimeographed.

———. "Experiencia piloto de gestión en las empresas de reforma agraria." Managua, 1983. Mimeographed.

———. "La generación neta de divisas del sector agrícola y agroindustrial de exportación." Managua, n.d. Mimeographed.

———. "Gestión de empresas de reforma agraria." Managua, 1984. Mimeographed.

———. "Información de base sobre las instancias de coordinación." Managua, 1982. Mimeographed.

———. *Informe de Nicaragua a la FAO.* Managua: MIDINRA, 1983.

———. "Intervención del comandante de la revolución Jaime Wheelock, en el seminario de propaganda directa." Managua, 1981. Mimeographed.

———. "Listas de empresas nacionales y de servicios adscritas a las direcciones centrales de MIDINRA y de sus principales actividades económicas al 30 de junio de 1983." Managua, 1983. Mimeographed.

———. "Manual de almacén." Managua, 1982. Mimeographed.

———. "Manual de inventario." Managua, n.d. Mimeographed.

———. "Manual de medios básicos." Managua, 1980. Mimeographed.

———. "Manual de organización empresa de agromecanización de reforma agraria: Agromec región II." Managua, n.d. Mimeographed.

———. "Marco estratégico del desarrollo agropecuario." Managua, 1983. Mimeographed.

———. "Marco estratégico del desarrollo agropecuario 1982–2000." Managua, 1983. Mimeographed.

———. Marco jurídico de la reforma agraria nicaragüense. Managua: MIDINRA, 1982.

———. Marco prospectivo del desarrollo agro-industrial. Vols. 1–2. Managua: MIDINRA, 1985.

———. "Metas de la producción agropecuaria: Requerimientos de factores y recursos 1982–1983." Managua, 1981. Mimeographed.

———. "Metodología del presupuesto: Empresas agropecuarias 1985–1986." Managua, 1985. Mimeographed.

———. "Metodología del sistema de estadísticas básicas (SEB)." Managua, 1984. Mimeographed.

———. La normación del trabajo. Managua: MIDINRA, 1985.

———. Las normas del trabajo en el sector agropecuario 1984–1985. Managua: MIDINRA, 1984.

———. "Plan técnico económico ciclo agrícola 1983–1984." Managua, 1982. Mimeographed.

———. Plan de trabajo 1985: Balance y perspectivas. Managua: MIDINRA, 1985.

———. Plan de trabajo 1987: Balance y perspectivas. Managua: MIDINRA, 1987.

———. "Política agropecuaria en Nicaragua 1981: Elementos para un diagnóstico de situación y propuestas metodológicas." Managua, 1981. Mimeographed.

———. "La política para el APP." Managua, 1982. Mimeographed.

———. "La política para los pequeños productores y para el semi-proletariado." Managua, 1982. Mimeographed.

————. "Las políticas para el sector agropecuario: Presentación por sector social." Managua, 1982. Mimeographed.

————. "Las políticas para el sector agropecuario: Presentación por subsistemas productivos." Managua, 1982. Mimeographed.

————. "Los problemas de fondo en el manejo reciente de la política agropecuaria." Managua, 1982. Mimeographed.

————. "Problemática de las empresas." Managua, 1985. Mimeographed.

————. "Problemática de las empresas del sector agropecuario adscritas al MIDINRA." Managua, 1985. Mimeographed.

————. "Relaciones comerciales entre las empresas agropecuarias adscritas a MIDINRA y a las empresas comercializadoras 1985." Managua, 1985. Mimeographed.

————. "Revisión integral de las empresas estatales agropecuarias y fortalecimiento de sus sistemas de dirección y gestión." Managua, n.d. Mimeographed.

————. Sector agropecuario: Resultados 1983 plan de trabajo 1984. Managua: MIDINRA, 1984.

————. "Síntesis del encuentro realizado entre MIDINRA y los trabajadores del tabaco." Managua, 1985. Mimeographed.

————. "Síntesis de sesiones de trabajo entre el ministerio de desarrollo agropecuario y reforma agraria comandante Jaime Wheelock Román y productores nacionales celebrada del 9 al 13 de mayo 1985." Managua, 1985. Mimeographed.

————. "Sistema de contabilidad de empresa." Managua, n.d. Mimeographed.

————. "Sistema de costo agro-industrial de tabaco." Managua, n.d. Mimeographed.

————. "Sistema de dirección de empresas." Managua, 1984. Mimeographed.

————. "Sistema de estadísticas." Managua, n.d. Mimeographed.

————. "Tres años de reforma agraria." Managua, 1982. Mimeographed.

————. "Una estrategia de riego de la planicie del pacífico de Nicaragua." Managua, 1985. Mimeographed.

————. "Validación de especificaciones técnicas según rubros de producción y niveles tecnológicos." Managua, 1984. Mimeographed.

Ministry of Planning (MIPLAN). Programa económico de austeridad y eficiencia 81. Managua: MIPLAN, 1981.

Ministry of State Farms Development. Untitled Report. Addis Ababa, 1985. Mimeographed.

Morawetz, David. "Economic Lessons from Some Small Socialist Developing Countries." *World Development* 8 (May–June 1980): 337–369.

National Autonomous University of Nicaragua (UNAN). Department of Social Sciences. *Curso sobre la problemática actual.* Managua: UNAN, 1980.

National Directorate of the Sandinista National Liberation Front (FSLN). "Análisis de la coyuntura y tareas de la revolución popular sandinista." Managua, 1979. Mimeographed.

National Reconstruction Government of Nicaragua. "Economic Policy Guidelines 1983–1988." Managua, n.d. Mimeographed.

National Secretary of Propaganda and Public Education of the FSLN. *Programa de reactivación económica en beneficio del pueblo.* Managua: National Secretary of Propaganda and Public Education of the FSLN, 1980.

———. *Propaganda de la producción.* Managua: National Secretary of Propaganda and Public Education of the FSLN, 1980.

Nicaraguan Association of Social Scientists (ANICS). *Estado y clases sociales en Nicaragua.* Managua: ANICS, 1982.

Nicaraguan Institute of Economic and Social Research (INIES). *Plan económico 1987.* Managua: INIES, 1987.

Ogliastri-Uribe, Enrique. "Estado, empresarios, sindicatos, trabajadores, administradores: Experiencias sobre gerencia y revolución en Nicaragua." Paper presented at the thirteenth international congress of Latin American Studies Association (LASA), Boston, October, 1986.

Pérez Palacios, Oscar. "Complejo agroindustrial de tabaco Burley: CATRA." Managua, n.d. Mimeographed.

Pinto, Julio César, and Edelberto Torres Rivas. *Problemas en la formación del estado nacional en Centroamérica.* San Jose: ICAP, 1983.

Pizarro, Roberto. "La nueva política económica en Nicaragua: Un reajuste necesario." *Economía de América Latina* 14 (1986): 75–91.

Pollitt, Brian. "The Transition to Socialist Agriculture in Cuba: Some Salient Features." *IDS Bulletin* 13 (1982): 12–22.

Portuondo Pichardo, Fernando M. *Economía de empresas industriales.* Vols. 1–2. Havana: Editorial Pueblo y Educación, 1985.

Rodríguez, Carlos Rafael. *Letra con filo.* Vol. 2. Havana: Editorial de Ciencias Sociales, 1983.

Rosengarten, Frederic, Jr. *Freebooters Must Die!* Wayne, Pa.: Haverford House, 1976.

Ruccio, David F. "The State and Planning in Nicaragua." In *The Politi-

*cal Economy of Revolutionary Nicaragua,* edited by Rose Spalding, pp. 61–82. Boston: Allen and Unwin, 1987.

Ruiz, Henry. "Dar un nuevo impulso a la economía nicaragüense." In *La revolución en Nicaragua: Ayer y hoy,* edited by Alexandr Sujostat, pp. 45–58. Moscow: Editorial Progreso, 1985.

Saprikova-Saminskaia, Tatiana. "Problemas económicos y vías para su solución." In *La revolución en Nicaragua: Ayer y hoy,* edited by Alexandr Sujostat, pp. 121–137. Moscow: Editorial Progreso, 1985.

Schurmann, Franz. *Ideology and Organization in Communist China.* Berkeley: University of California Press, 1968.

Secretariat of Planning and Budget (SPP). "Empleo e ingreso rural agropecuario." Managua, 1985. Mimeographed.

———. *Plan económico nacional 1986.* Managua, 1986. Mimeographed.

Serra, Luis. "Capacitación, organización popular y democracia en Nicaragua." Managua, 1985. Mimeographed.

Sichiev, N. G. *Finanzas de las empresas y ramas de la economía nacional.* Havana: Editorial Pueblo y Educación, 1985.

Somerville, Keith. *Angola.* London: Frances Pinter, 1986.

Torres, Rosa María, and José Luis Corragio. *Transición y crisis en Nicaragua.* San Jose: DEI, 1987.

Union of Nicaraguan Agricultural Producers (UPANIC). "Estudios económicos." Managua, 1983. Mimeographed.

Vilas, Carlos M. "Troubles Everywhere: An Economic Perspective on the Sandinista Revolution." In *The Political Economy of Revolutionary Nicaragua,* edited by Rose Spalding, pp. 233–246. Boston: Allen and Unwin, 1987.

Warnken, Philip. *The Agricultural Development of Nicaragua.* Columbia: University of Missouri Press, 1975.

Wheelock, Jaime. *Entre la crisis y la agresión: La reforma agraria sandinista.* Managua: MIDINRA, 1984.

Yañez, Eugenio. *Complejos agroindustriales y desarrollo económico.* Havana: Editorial Científico-Técnica, 1985.

Zelaya, José M. *El estado sandinista.* Managua: Editorial Unión, 1985.

## Nicaraguan Newspapers and Magazines

*Barricada*
*Cuadernos empresariales*
*Encuentro*
*Envío*

*Informaciones agropecuarias*
*Marxista leninista*
*El Nuevo Diario*
*Patria libre*
*Pensamiento propio*
*Revolución y desarrollo*
*El Socialista*

## Cuban Newspaper

*Granma Weekly Review*

# Index